LOCAL HISTORY

A
Little Boy's
War

Roy Bartlett

authorHOUSE™

1663 LIBERTY DRIVE, SUITE 200
BLOOMINGTON, INDIANA 47403
(800) 839-8640
WWW.AUTHORHOUSE.COM

First published by AuthorHouse 5/5/2006

ISBN: 1-4208-8916-8 (sc)

Printed in the United States of America
Bloomington, Indiana

This book is printed on acid-free paper.

DEDICATION

In loving memory of my parents Edwin (Tom) and Mary. Their indomitable spirit and strength of character inspired my life

ACKNOWLEDGEMENTS

Wartime photographs by kind permission of the Middlesex County Times (Ealing Gazette) The London Borough of Ealing Central Library Local History Centre and the Gunnersbury Park Museum

FOREWORD

WARTIME BRITAIN.
LIFE ON THE HOME FRONT

For the past 49 consecutive nights we had endured the incessant drone of enemy aircraft, the thud of anti-aircraft fire and shudder of nearby bombs.

A nerve tingling background that had almost become normality to the conscious mind.

Suddenly, on the night of September 27th 1940 this was shattered by a tremendous exploding crescendo of noise and fiery glare like Dante's Inferno as a bomb struck somewhere very close.

This is the story of an ordinary family throughout the dark days of war torn Britain, related through the eyes of a young lad.

This narrative has been compiled over a number of years. Retirement allowed the time and inclination to collate a collection of notes and memories into sequence. My original scruffy school exercise book diary, letters and other records left by family members. Anecdotes related by living relatives, but above all, vivid memories that will never fade.

Were those days so traumatic to a young person that they became deeply engrained, enabling the whole scenario to now be recalled as virtual reality?

Enhanced by dramatic and sometimes tragic circumstances, an indelible imprint is thereby assured.

I may now forget what happened last week, but so easily recall names and events of those days, in particular, the German Luftwaffe 'Blitz' on London in 1940.

Little evidence now remains of those gaping bomb craters and grotesque piles of rubble that were commonplace. Some clues are still apparant, but only to those who know. The passage of time is inexorably fading the last vestiges of visual history.

The site of what may be termed 'Our bomb' was left as a cleared site for many years, sacrosanct to the memory of a family whose remains were never found. Eventually, new shops were built to finally eradicate a scene of tragedy that to me, could have occurred just last week.

There are not too many of us left now in the category of living history. It is so vitally important that younger generations have access to some realistic record to which they may relate and understand just what happened all those years ago.

Events which shaped their own destiny, freedom and a way of life that may be enjoyed today.

The debt that is owed to their forebears is incalculable.

LIFE ON THE HOME FRONT

For many months I had overheard my parents, brothers and sister, talking about the prospects of war. Always in hushed tones, but names such as the Rhineland, Austria, Herr Hitler and Chamberlain were becoming increasingly familiar to me.

However, to a lad of nine, such serious chit-chat was merely an intrusion upon the really important things in life, such as how many goals I scored in the playground kick-abouts, or the adventures of Tarzan at Saturday morning pictures.

Another diversion was to see how far we could push the patience of our new lady teacher, who had a mannerism totally fascinating to impressionable young lads. Her very ample bosom would heave up and down with increasing tempo as her anger welled. We all contemplated the prospect of these bumps flying into orbit around the classroom, having no idea how firmly fixed they were.

The implications of war was something that could only be fully grasped by the older generation, who had experienced and could so readily recall the sheer bloody holocaust of the 1914/18 war just 21 years earlier. To me, all this chatter and speculation merely heralded some exciting interlude.

We lived in Ealing, a West London suburb that in the thirties was known as the 'Queen of the Suburbs'. A well laid out pleasant locality with an abundance of parks and common land, yet with thriving industry to provide employment for the working classes, in what was then, a class conscious society.

Some parts of Ealing were very posh, where tradesmen were still expected to call at the back door. I look at some of those fine houses now, converted into multiple flats and housing a diversity of ethnic groups and wonder just what the original owners would have to say.

My parents, Tom and Mary, struggled to achieve a decent living from a hardware stores in South Ealing. This sold virtually everything for the household. A veritable Aladdin's cave of mystery, with shelves and cubby holes intriguingly labelled Lamp Black, Shellac, Black Lead, Pumice Stone, Red Ochre and other weird names.

Dad always assured me that the Pumice Stone was genuine lava from the slopes of Vesuvius. There were many other strange things common to use in those days.

My father had served in the army during the first great war of 1914/18, but was fortunate to have missed the horrendous battlefields of France and Belgium.

He saw active service in the Middle East region of Mesopotamia, now known as Iran and Iraq.

He said very little about this episode in his life, but was proud of the fact that at sometime he had shaken the hand of the famous 'Lawrence of Arabia', the British officer who organised and led an Arab revolt against the enemy Turkish forces.

I loved to sneak a look into a colourful tin 'goodies' box that was hidden away. This contained his campaign medals which are now in my possession. There was also a faded envelope which contained a fragile dried up leaf, captioned 'From the tree of knowledge', wherever that may be!

A number of sepia toned photographs showed dad leaning against various palm trees, resplendent in his tropical uniform complete with a white pith helmet.

Rattling around in the bottom of the tin box was a motley assortment of coins, cap badges and various other bits and pieces that obviously represented memories.

One outstanding item always caught my eye. A three diamond gold ring. On one occasion I was caught in the act of rummaging, but dad was okay about it and said "Do you like that ring?, it means a lot to me, but when you are 21 it's yours".

True to his word, I was thrilled to receive it on my birthday. Having then worn it for some 25 years I duly passed it on to my son Gordon on his 'Coming of age'. I like to think that in due course it will again be passed on to my grandson Craig.

Coming up to a verifiable 100 years old, it is a fascinating but unanswerable question as to its Middle Eastern origin

As I grew older I could understand that after his return to 'Civvy Street' life was difficult. Many men could not find employment. Dad was no exception, yet still had a family to feed. My mother took in washing and ironing, or any other mundane task that would fetch in a few shillings.

Eventually dad got a job 'on the dust' as it was termed. Humping the heavy old metal dustbins from back-yards to empty the household waste into the back of an open smelly lorry full of unmentionable matter. What a far cry from the clean hygenic plastic sacks of today!

Eventually, he progressed – if that is the right word, to work at a large sewerage disposal plant in South Ealing.

What he actually did remains a mystery, nobody went near enough to ask him!

My future wife's father fought in the muddy, bloody horror of the trenches on the Somme in 1915, just a few months after joining up. Within a few short weeks he was back in 'Blighty' minus a leg. Hearing a wounded comrade crying out for water he wriggled nearer to throw his water bottle. As he did so, a burst of machine gun fire tore into his leg.

3

Roy Bartlett

A seemingly endless succession of operations concluded with the fitment of a heavy cumbersome harness arrangement to manipulate a false wooden leg. Despite this, he led a full life and for many years undertook his employment as a night watchman at a factory in Brentford. He even cycled everywhere with his faithful dog Judy sitting in the rear pannier.

I can still picture him dancing at our wedding.

Gradually my parents scraped together enough money to take a lease on the shop in 1936 and so, for the first time in their hard lives, gained independence and the opportunity to prosper by personal enterprise.

Trade must have been difficult. I can well remember dad setting off with a barrow to collect fallen tree branches from the local parks. These were sawn up to sell as fire logs or sticks.

Sunday mornings became a ritual. He would sit at a wooden chopping block wielding an axe to make up piles of uniform length sticks. Mother would then stack and pull into neat round bundles by means of a wooden lever contraption to be tied with tarred string.

Sunday dinner was invariably preceded by a family 'chain gang' pitching the bundles one to another down the garden path and into the shop container.

We lived above the premises. The house itself was an adventure playground that my mates loved to visit.

A cellar beneath was favourite, but forbidden territory. That only added to the thrill as we crept quietly down the creaky wooden stairs, wedging the door shut behind us, to explore this cold dank area where my brother Ted had a workbench to produce beautiful furniture for his future home.

He had the rather unusual occupation as butler in one of the fine houses. Rather illogical in view of his obvious talent with wood.

The building comprised four stories, with sets of stairs totalling 36 treads to the top floor, where the front bedroom allowed access to a parapet by climbing through a window.

This area provided a panoramic view across the London skyline.

On a clear day the dome of St Paul's Cathedral was clearly visible and with a bit of neck stretching and binoculars, the top of 'Big Ben'.

Little did we know then what incredible scenes were to be witnessed from that viewpoint in the years to come.

All the talk at school was about some strange activity known as evacuation should war actually break out. As far as I could figure out this meant that you left home to live with complete strangers in a far away place that no-one must mention, yet they reckoned you would have a great time!

I was not impressed and decided to ignore the whole silly affair.

My mother would certainly not admit so, but I guess was rather relieved when I announced "Don't care if you do 'ave me on this vaciation lark, I aint goin'".

The first time that I can actually recall being frightened at the prospect of war was when gasmasks arrived at the school and we were required to line up for fittings. It was now personal.

Ugh!, that horrible pungent smell of new rubber and the claustrophobic stifled breathing as the masks were slipped over our heads for the first time. How pleased I was that the cellular window quickly misted over to hide my tears.

"Breathe in" commanded the very bossy lady instructor. We dutifully sucked in filtered air through the pig like snout. "Now out" she cried. Then to the intense delight of all kids, if you blew hard enough the expelled air spluttered out from the side of one's face below the ears with a resounding 'Raspberry' sound.

This gave the proceedings a competitive edge as we vied for supremacy in a cacophony of rude sounds, totally ignoring the frantic cries of the boss lady trying to restore some order.

We returned home proudly clutching our square cardboard boxes with string shoulder straps that would not last the proverbial five minutes. These masks were to become our constant companions for at least the next two years.

During that time ingenuity prevailed as cloth or leather cases were home-made to replace the already tatty remnants of the original boxes. Some cylindrical tin canisters became available.

The wireless as it was known, became the focal point of home life as families gathered around their sets to listen to every news bulletin, which alternated between optimism or gloom as this fellow Hitler ranted and raved and began to impose his will.

My job of carrying the wireless accumulators to the local shop for re-charging became increasingly regular.

The German armies had marched across the frontier of Czechoslovakia in March 1939 and it became increasingly obvious that Britains policy of softly-softly appeasement was having little effect to evil intent.

Britain and France made a joint pledge to Poland that if Germany invaded that country we would immediately go to their aid. It was anticipated that this declaration would be sufficient to deter Hitler from any more 'smash and grab' raids.

A forlorn hope. On September 1st 1939 the fateful news came through that Germany had defied this ultimatum and launched a fierce unprovoked attack on Poland.

Even I could now understand the gravity of the situation. The mood was very sombre. Grown-ups were going about their business with very long faces and short tempers as they contemplated the inevitable outcome.

A few black beetle like Barrage Balloons now appeared in the sky over London. I first thought that someone held them on a length of rope until realising just how huge they were.

In accordance with Civil Defence recommendations and with a pessimistic foresight, work had already started way back in 1938 to excavate trenches in all the local parks and open spaces. Some brick built roadside shelters were popping up in some of the side roads. These did not appear to be very substantial, but better than nothing in an emergency.

Now, all this work became a matter of urgency and swarms of workmen, including the unemployed, worked feverishly to complete the projects, whilst others filled innumerable sandbags, aided by volunteer labour.

All non essential building work was put on hold to boost the labour force.

My father had been rather shrewd in stocking up with reels of sticky paper tape which were quickly snapped up by customers as advice came over the wireless to cover all windows with criss-cross designs to minimise the effect of flying glass from bomb blast. There was also a mesh fabric that could be glued to the glass. This was preferable, but in very short supply and dad failed in this quest.

I helped my sister Ivy to do all the many windows in a diamond pattern with an additional strip across the middle. This seemed to be neat and hopefully effective.

It was all becoming very real now as the air-raid sirens were constantly tested and we became familiar with that chilling wail that sent shivers down the spine. 'Moaning Minnie' became an inevitable nickname.

One of my clearest recollections is standing at the back door with mother assuring me 'It's only a practice, they won't really need them', then watching in amazement as my tabby cat Stripey hurtled over the garden fence to shoot between our legs and cower under the scullery sink!. That was to become his ritual every time the sirens sounded. I guess that by comparison to his nocturnal prowling howl he must have thought 'That's got to be one helluva big moggie out there!'

In fact he became something of an early warning system when he came racing indoors before the local sirens sounded. They say that cat's hearing is nine times that of a human, so he must have heard distant warnings.

Came that fateful Sunday morning, September 3rd 1939. We were all aware that there was to be an important announcement by the Prime Minister – Neville Chamberlain at 11.00am Lawn mowers were abandoned, Sunday dinners put on hold and the entire nation hushed as the time approached.

Our family gathered in the kitchen as dad fiddled with the crackling wireless. Come on dad we urged, as the sound of 'Big Ben' came through. Then, anti-climax, the broadcast was delayed until 11.15am.

The Prime Minister eventually spoke in quiet, tremulous tones as millions hung upon his every word, concluding "No such undertaking has been received, consequently I have to tell you that this country is now at war with Germany".

I was the baby of the family with fourteen years difference between me and my brother Bernard. Why I was referred to as the mistake was beyond my comprehension!

Mum's arm was round my shoulder during the broadcast. I felt her stiffen as she softly muttered "Oh my God.- Not again!"

As the family sat in reflective silence dad broke the tension. "Oh well, that's it. Better get on with it now I suppose".

As we dispersed to do our own things the sirens sounded for the first time in reality. We listened intently for the expected roar of aero engines but it remained deathly quiet until we heard a clatter against our front door. Some poor lady, overcome by the situation had chosen our doorway to throw a faint!

Whilst all this was going on there was an almighty crash from the back yard. Incredibly, our neighbours metal rainwater pipe had chosen that inopportune moment to fall off the wall.

Whilst my sister attended to the fainted lady we stood around contemplating the situation until we heard a groaning sound from over the fence. Bern pulled himself up to peer over.

"Oh gawd, it's whacked him one!" he exclaimed.

The old chap who lived next door was lying on the ground, the pipe which he had been trying to repair had caught him a glancing blow to the head.

With the name of Zeebak and of suspected German origin, Bern said "Might as well leave him there now, one down already!"

I can still hear mum exclaiming "Bernard, don't say things like that, it's not kind!"

Unfortunately, kindness would not be very prominent in the years ahead.

With the fainted lady on her feet again, mum clambered over the fence to attend to our bleeding neighbour- which in the circumstances seemed to be fair comment.

By now, we had almost forgotten that there was supposed to be a raid on and were surprised to hear the All-Clear sound.

London had in fact been given it's baptism by a solitary British aircraft wandering about the sky.

Improvised black-out arrangements had already been made to comply with a full scale practice way back in August, but now it was for real. Ingenuity was the keynote as my mother and sister set-to cutting up dark blue blankets to make light-proof curtains for the main rooms. Little did they know that these would prove to be possible life savers.

In lesser used rooms the electric light bulbs were removed to prevent thoughtless switching on. My brothers were busy cutting out snug fitting sheets of wood to fit permanently over little used windows and discussing whilst doing so, the inevitability of their call-up to the armed forces.

Even torches had to be shrouded or masked with tape until only a slit of light showed.

Metal buckets from the shop stock were filled with sand or water and placed strategically around the house. My parents were particularly concerned that in an outhouse behind the shop they had two fifty gallon Paraffin oil storage tanks. The only cover was a flimsy glass roof which was not a very comforting thought.

Recalling that there was only one bucket of each, sand and water, to constitute the entire fire precautions for that area, I guess that faith and optimism were somewhat stretched!

Within a short while the buckets were complimented by the arrival of a stirrup pump. This was a simple two legged contraption with a pumping handle. The idea was, that one leg was placed in the bucket – yours or the pump being optional! One of a twosome pumped the handle vigorously up and down, whilst the other crawled forward like a demented crab, hose in one hand and a dustbin lid for protection in the other. This antic was very rough on both knees and elbows and generally delegated to the youngest.

There was a choice of jet for burning materials, or a fine misty spray that hopefully obliterated an actual incendiary bomb by exhausting the air supply. We remained to be convinced!

The down-side was of course, that a bucket of water would not last very long, an aspect that would become critical in the days ahead.

In due course, large canvas or metal portable reservoirs were to become a familiar sight on street corners or any spare land, usually plastered with posters proclaiming a great example of unwitting humour – 'Fall in the firebomb fighters'.

Meanwhile, at school everything was now being geared up for this evacuation nonsense taking place the following Sunday.

With foresight that any future war would involve mass air attacks endangering the civilian population, the government had drawn up basic evacuation plans as early as 1931.

Whilst there was still no direct threat of war, more comprehensive schedules were prepared and released in 1933.

Such a massive logistical operation was projected to commence 72 hours prior to any anticipated outbreak of hostilities.

As the political situation in Europe worsened, by November 1938 the evacuation plans were firmed up, together with activation of an A.R.P. (Air Raid Precautions) organization.

In addition, 44 million gasmasks had been produced and stockpiled for localized distribution.

What a fantastic masterpiece of efficient pre-planning!

When planning became reality in early September 1939, operation 'Pied Piper' as it was called, went smoothly into operation with scarcely a hitch, involving the initial movement of 200.000 children, nursing and expectant mothers, blind people and helpers. Over the next few days the exodus continued, involving the use of 4000 trains, 200.000 buses and even coastal paddle steamers.

As the operation drew to a close, an incredible 3½ million children and others had been transported to places of safety away from the vunerable cities.

Obviously, there must have been minor 'hiccups' along the way, but it is generally recognised that this 'mind boggling' undertaking was accomplished as planned and with no recorded major problem.

I cannot help pondering as to whether such a complex operation could be formulated and carried out in our present time.

For some reason, our school was in 'Phase Z' whatever that means. We went towards the end of the operation. The majority of London kids had already disappeared.

In the meantime, it had dawned upon me that despite my original misgivings I had become the only one in my class who was not going!

This put an entirely different outlook on the situation. I could not face that lonely prospect, or the teacher who said "If you think that I am going to teach you on your own, you have another think coming".

Mum said "I don't really like the idea of you going away, anyway, last week you didn't want to go".

Contrary as kids can be, that no longer counted and I have vague recollections of throwing a wobbly.

The situation eased somewhat when my best friend's mother was co-opted as a helper and undertook to look after my interests in getting us billeted together.

I was dusted down, scrubbed and polished to perfection for this momentous journey into the unknown. It is so difficult now to comprehend the anguish that parents must have felt in letting their 'little darlings' undertake this adventure to wherever and more importantly, to whom.

As we assembled outside the school gates we examined a new post that had been erected with a dull green painted board screwed to the top. Beneath this a notice proclaimed 'In the event of a gas attack this board will change colour'.

What it omitted to say, was what colour the board would take, or advise the bystander that should they hang around long enough for this phenomenon to take place, they too would change colour!

We all gathered with increasing excitement which rather overcame our fears and trepidation. Emotional goodbyes took place all around. Tears flowed profusely as all the mum's cried out 'Don't forget to write – Be good – Wash behind your ears – Change your socks' and all the other platitudes that mothers are famed for.

I remember my mother trying desperately to stem the tears and assure me that I would be with nice people and would have a great time. Dad stood to one side with all the other fathers. In those days it was not the done thing for men to show any emotion.

We had all been tagged with large labels tied to our jacket lapels proclaiming our name and school. We clambered aboard London double-decker buses as red as our eyes, fiercely clutching our small suitcases, gas-masks and a carrier bag of 'goodies'.

Our destination remained a top secret, but reputedly a long way. This was substantiated when a packed lunch was distributed by the helpers and teachers.

To this day, I cannot help smiling for we finished up at a place called Wooburn Green, a village in Buckinghamshire, just 24 miles away, although to us, the journey had seemed for ever. In later life I worked near Maidenhead and drove the same distance there and back every day.

In the village hall we were sorted out like so many bundles of washing. It seemed to me that little girls were the first choice, presumably with the logic that they would be less trouble than us 'Cockney' boys as we were termed.

Gradually the numbers thinned. On current reflection I wonder why Ken and I were among the 'left-overs'. Surely someone should have picked out such sweet faced angelic little lads!

Maybe Ken's mother was being selective on our behalf but she was not around when we were bundled into a car to be touted around the village on offer.

Within a 100 yards the car stopped and it remains one of the most vivid memories of my life, sitting in the back scared stiff. We huddled together in the back seat, school caps askew and gazed out on a sea of faces peering in through the windows and discussing our merits.

"Don't 'e look pale – Poor little soul". Was that me or Ken? "Aaaaah, poor little Lunnoners - Oos goin' to 'ave these two then?"

The accents were strange, we must be hundreds of miles from home. We sniffed back the tears. Perhaps we would never see our homes ever again.

Gradually the hubbub eased and a kindly smiling couple opened the car door and said quietly "Hello boys, would you like to come and stay with us?"

We were not sure about anything, but how could we say no? Nodding meekly we slowly trudged behind them up a long garden path towards a neat looking bungalow.

So commenced a friendship with Connie and Bill that was to last more than 60 years and turn full cycle when Bill became Godfather to my own son Gordon, eighteen years after that fateful morning.

As we entered the bungalow our eyes immediately alighted on a gleaming brass helmet hanging in the hall, topping all the obvious equipment of a fireman. Our now eager questions broke the ice as Bill explained that he was a part-time fireman in the voluntary service and that the village engine was kept in a shed virtually at the end of the garden. Things were looking up!

An electric bell hung silently on the wall despite the combined mental powers of Ken and myself to activate the thing. This was going to be a real test of patience.

Connie told me in later years that the 'goodies' bag we clutched contained a tin of 'Bully' (Corned) Beef, a packet of biscuits and a pot of jam which we insisted were for our first meal. The teachers told us! Just how one combined 'Bully Beef, jam and biscuits is quite beyond me.

Inwardly chuckling but happy to indulge our whim, Connie sensibly suggested opening just one tin to share. "No! Can't do that, we must each have our own tin!

I can just imagine Connie and Bill thinking 'Good grief, what have we let ourselves in for'.

We always wondered whether it was purely co-incidental that midway though lunch and within half an hour of our arrival, the bells 'went down'. We sat spellbound by the thrill of it all as Connie held out each piece of equipment in the right order for Bill to dive into, then watch him race down the garden path buttoning his tunic and axe belt with one hand, helmet swinging in the other.

How totally disappointed we were when he quickly returned from a practice 'turn-out'.

Outside, there seemed to be a lot of garden space with chickens roaming about. "Don't chase them" said Bill. "If you do, no eggs for breakfast". We were impressed, this man could also read our thoughts.

I have been told that later that first day a suggested bath became a problem. We refused to take our clothes off and when finally persuaded to do so, hid behind the end of the bath. No way was this strange lady going to see our bits and pieces!

Connie and Bill had only been married for a year and the sudden adoption of two young lads from London subsequently proved too much to handle. We could not have been easy.

Ken was the first to go after just a few weeks. His mother found new 'Digs' in Maidenhead, which left me feeling rather lonely and vunerable.

The sudden mass influx of Cockney kids as we were termed, put a strain on the hitherto quiet and peaceful community and the limited educational facilities.

As a temporary measure we were accommodated in the village hall. This episode in my academic life made little or no impression, with only scant recall of the teachers or environment.

The winter of 1939/40 was quite severe and the one achievement that does come to mind, is chucking a snowball high onto the tall sloping roof of the adjacent Methodist church, then watching in gratified amazement and horror as the snow layer cracked across, gathered speed and avalanched down into the playground totally obliterating a very bossy obnoxious little girl standing beneath. My fame and popularity were instantly assured.

Every morning we would dash en-masse across the village green, envoking the wrath of any teacher witnessing this mass escape. We were off to the nearby railway level crossing in order to watch the 'Namer' thunder through just before 9.00am. Would it be a 'Castle Class' or perhaps the name of some noble lord glimpsed through the hissing soot laden whoosh of steam.

The more daring lads – not me of course – would place a halfpenny on the rail to later retrieve a larger but much thinner coin.

My parents visited as often as possible on a Sunday, travelling part way by bus, but often walking many miles. There were very few private cars about and petrol was severely rationed. Sometimes they were lucky to pick up a lift, usually in a lorry.

I recall one visit when dad arrived with a black face. They had been given a lift in a coal lorry and with only room for mum in the cab, poor old dad had to sit in the open back.

Gradually a firm and lasting friendship was established between my real and stand-in parents that stood the test of time until deaths in later years.

The months passed by and the anticipated mass air attacks on London had not materialised. Indeed, the lack of activity in Europe led the Americans to term this 'The Phoney War'.

My first Christmas away from home was made as happy as possible. My parents were not able to come down for some reason or another but had brought my presents the previous week.

Toys and the like were becoming scarce, but as a 9 year old, who wanted toys anyway. Certainly not from 'Santa'!

Connie and Bill gave me a set of Draughts, an annual book and a Solitaire set.

Incredibly, the draughts set is now part of an impressive collection of wartime memorabilia amassed by Connie's grandson who is the historian for the Wooburn Green Fire Brigade. He is also the proud owner of three vintage, but immaculately restored fire appliances from the wartime era. These are now in demand for various prestigious parades and wartime films.

It is sad that the original engine that I was so happy to play on in 1939/40 totally disappeared from all records and must have been scrapped at some time.

The restored appliances are currently garaged at the end of the garden, only yards from the site of the original fire station.

With a very protective mother and equally so foster mum, I stood little chance and was cosseted like a rare flower, but Pansy comes more readily to mind!

Every morning I had to endure a dose of Caster Oil, together with a spoonful of some weird concoction called 'Angiers Emulsion', a 1930s version of preventative medicine. Ugh!, a thick yellow gunge far more likely to make one sick.

I also had to suffer thick woolen vests and underpants that I dare not reveal to the village kids. P.E. lessons were a real problem, entailing a sneaky visit to the toilet to remove and hide them before the session.

Many of the kids were now returning home. Generally they were happy in the countryside but parents were missing them and seeking excuses to bring them home. Everyone had been lulled into a false sense of security, for not one German bomber had ventured over London – Yet!.

As new found friends gradually disappeared, classes at the village hall became smaller, until with just a few of us left we were transferred to the 'Proper' school to become outcasts among the village lads. The term 'Cockney kid' became one of derision.

Evidently a similar situation was being repeated all over the country and considerable problems were being created in the cities. No-one had foreseen that the evacuation scheme would break down so quickly. It was confidently expected to last for the duration of the war.

Consequently, many schools had been shut down and for an interim period kids were running the streets until sufficient teachers and staff could be recruited to re-open premises.

Many were elderly retired men and women who were dragged screaming and kicking out of peace and tranquility and back to reality.

As mentioned, my foster mum Connie was very protective and we had many a verbal battle when she would not allow me to take my football boots to school on games day should there be the slightest hint of rain "You will get your feet wet and catch a chill" was the cry. No problem! All I did was to leave the boots 'handy' and the window on the latch. Then creep back under window level on hands and knees, reach in and steal them away.

I never did find out where it all came from, but virtually every day for one meal or another, we would have a Pineapple chunks. I was never very partial to them, so after a while the very sight became nausiating. I was threatened and cajoled "Eat them up, they are good for you".

To this day I hate Pineapple! Some years ago I was seated next to a lady mayor at a function. The sweet was fresh fruit salad inevitably containing this fruit. Despite careful sorting, a piece found it's way into my mouth. Decorum was preserved by a discreet cough into my handkerchief.

After dinner and whilst chatting to this gracious lady, without thinking I pulled out the 'hanky again. 'Plop'. Out fell the offending piece to bobble along the floor in full view. Squirming, all I could think of to say was "Goodness me, what was that? , I do hope it did not fall off your chain of office" Whilst she examined the regalia a swift kick under the table removed the evidence.

By May 1940 my brief experience as a 'Country Bumpkin' came to an end. Just prior to my 10th birthday I too returned home, having been away just 9 months.

I was not told at the time, it would not have been a subject for discussion, but I subsequently found out that Connie was pregnant. Looking after me and a baby would not have been a welcome or intended prospect therefore my return was by way of mutual agreement.

We were so naive in those days that I suspect my only query would have been 'How did that happen?'

Whilst I had been away both my brothers had been called-up to the armed forces. Bernard joined the Royal Army Service Corps and Ted the R.A.F. as ground staff.

Everything was changing so fast. The caretaker of Little Ealing schools had been called-up to the Royal Navy. My father became his replacement. I was not too happy about the prospect of dad hovering about all the time.

The premises comprised three separate buildings spread over a wide area, built some 35 years earlier to cater for the rapidly expanding residential area.

Consequently, the schools were able to cater for a child's entire academic education with adjacent Primary, Junior and Senior sections.

Under our shop the storage cellar had been converted into a public air-raid shelter capable of accommodating 12 sleeping people when double bunks were installed. Doorways were knocked through into adjoining cellars to create additional escape routes. There was one exception however, no door into the bank. I wonder why?

Strong timber uprights supported a thick secondary roof. All the additional timber was secured with huge bolts and grappling irons. It looked strong, but it would have to be to support the collapse of a three storey house above.

Pavement entrances descended almost vertically down wooden steps. A metal cover could be closed over the entrance 'hole' and a round ventilator section screwed up tight in the event of a gas attack.

Initially, many of our regular guests preferred the more civilised way in via our front door, but eventually got used to the 'tradesmens entrance' as it was termed. In the days ahead it was often standing room only down there.

Despite all efforts to make the cellar more comfortable, it was cold, damp and airless, with an ever present smell of carbolic from the single Elsan bucket toilet in one corner, screened only by heavy hessian curtains.

In due course, people acquired the art of controlling bodily functions until obscured by gunfire or aircraft!.

For 'private' or domestic protection the authorities had encouraged those families with basements or suitable downstairs rooms to have them strengthened as indoor shelters.

Instruction leaflets were distributed and even a set of cigarette cards entitled 'Air Raid Precautions'.

However, few of the modern 1930s houses, or the prevailing Edwardian terrace style in Ealing, had basements.

Consequently, a cheap and simple shelter was freely distributed to low income families, but at a charge of £7 to the more affluent. This was known as the 'Anderson'. Some say named after the designer Dr David Anderson, others that it took the name of the Home Secretary, Sir John Anderson.

Original thinking was, that these could be erected indoors to provide protection for 6 people.

In the event, virtually all the Andersons were erected in back gardens, where I suspect a few remain to this day.

Basically they were similar in shape to the present day portable canvas workmens hut, usually erected over holes in the pavement.

A large hole was excavated and the corrugated curved steel sections were lowered up to two thirds deep into the ground, then bolted together.

The earth removed was then piled back over the top together with any surplus from elsewhere. The more the better.

Obviously, the deeper they were embedded the more protection they afforded. Handy-men made doors for them, but these had to be left ajar for ventilation. At the very least it was recommended that a heavy blanket be hung across the entrance. In the event of a gas attack this could then be soaked with water.

The usual form of lighting and a little additional warmth, was a Paraffin oil Hurricane Lamp. If people did not have a portable oil stove, then a candle inside an upturned flower pot had to suffice. For personal comfort it was the good old hot water bottle.

The Andersons proved to have an excellent resistance to anything but a direct hit or near miss. A major drawback apart from the cold was that they were prone to flooding and also provided a cosy haven for spiders and field mice. Many women were more scared of them than Hitler's bombs!

Equipped with bunk beds, many families spent months of consecutive nights 'down the hole' and they undoubtedly saved many lives.

An 'emergency' bag or attache case would be taken down, containing important documents, ration books, money and any other valuables. If the house was destroyed at least some essentials would be safe.

Installation was of course, really hard graft, particularly for the womenfolk left at home. The shelter had to be completed as soon as possible so it was essential for people to 'muck in' and help each other to complete the task. In the meantime neighbours would share a shelter until others were completed.

It had been ominously quiet, except at sea. No anticipated air-raids and little activity on the mainland of Europe. There was a strange feeling of optimism that perhaps after all, there might be some form of peaceful settlement.

This illusion was soon to be shattered.

On May 10th 1940, German Panzer Divisions rolled into France and Belgium despite the intervention of a hastily assembled British Expeditionary force. Belgium was forced to surrender on May 28th. The Allied armies were forced back across France in the face of an onslought by overwhelming forces, but finally turned disaster into triumph by the incredible evacuation from Dunkirk that rescued some 334.000 British and Allied troops, thanks to the heroic efforts of the Royal Navy and the now famous armada of 'Little ships', owned and in many cases crewed by volunteer, so called, 'Sunday Sailors'.

Within days, France capitulated to leave Britain standing alone against the German might, with just 21 miles of water between us.

The English Channel proved to be our greatest ally as the populace braced itself for a seemingly inevitable invasion onslought. The general expectation was, that this would take the form of a massive air attack, followed by parachute troop landings in support of a coastal beach assault.

Surely, this just had to happen. Britain was totally unprepared and Hitler must know that.

We now know that at that time there was only one Canadian Division in England that was fully equipped. Virtually all other arms and equipment had been destroyed and left in France.

Our new Prime Minister, Winston Churchill made an inspiring broadcast to the nation, concluding "We shall fight them on the beaches, we shall fight them in the streets, on the landing grounds and in the hills. We shall defend our island whatever the cost may be. We shall never surrender".

Frantic defence measures were being implemented. Local Defence volunteers, subsequently known as the 'Home Guard' or 'Dad's Army' were being recruited from the too old, too young, or those unfit for the regular forces but still keen to 'ave a bash.

It was an exciting diversion for me to watch them being drilled in the school playground each evening. They were armed with a motley collection of 'weapons'. Broom handles were utilised as rifles for drill, reminding one of Robin Hood and his merry men. One or two lucky one's had their own sporting shotgun or air rifle.

Within a few weeks they were thrilled to receive a supply of old rifles, possibly stored in thick grease since the first world war. I seem to remember that just 5 rounds of ammunition was initially supplied.

The spirit and determination was very apparent but I doubt that this brave intrepid band would have fared well against fully equipped paratroops.

Initially, dad's work as caretaker of a virtually empty school was 'Cushy'. The kids remaining after the evacuation had been accommodated in other schools as an intended long term measure. However, as evacuees began to return home in increasing numbers, the premises re-opened with a rather decrepit staff hastily recruited to impart wisdom to all us little horrors. Meanwhile, large air-raid shelters had been excavated in two of the three playgrounds, capable of accomodating some 200 children. Cloakrooms were also strengthened to provide additional protection.

Every possible inch of soil was being cultivated for food crops. The huge mounds now covering the underground shelters were no exception. Dad scattered marrow seeds all over the earth and merely raked them in. 'Green fingers' had a challenge!

However, he was the one with a grin on his face as creeping tendrils began to cover the earth with greenery.

B' COMPANY. 2nd BATTALION MIDDLESEX HOME GUARD AUTOMATIC SECTION WITH THE MEN AT THE REAR PULLING BROWNING MACHINE GUNS.MARCHING THROUGH EALING ON THE 15th MARCH 1942.BY THEN, THE IMMEDIATE DANGER OF INVASION HAD PASSED AND THE HOME GUARD UNITS WERE REASONABLY WELL EQUIPPED.

NOTE THE WHITE RINGS AROUND THE TREE TO AID TRAVELLERS IN THE BLACK-OUT

Photograph by kind permission of Gunnersbury Park Museum

In due course his 'King size' marrows were really something and distributed fairly among the staff.

My mother concocted some imaginary dishes that even extended to marrow jam!

I helped dad after school hours by shutting all the large sash windows with a long pole and then baling out the water pits beneath the floor of the underground playground shelters. Being so deeply constructed they were affected by the water table.

In the early days this was a thankless task of hard graft as we only had buckets to lug up and down the fourteen steps.

Later installation of a water pump made the job more appealing but still hard work. This was a hand cranked contraption with a push-pull handle to suck the water up over 30 feet to flow away down the playground. Didn't like that job!

On second thoughts, it did have compensations. On several occasions during the winter I became a very popular lad by squirting the outflow over an expanse of the playground to provide a super ice rink by next morning.

The reaction of the headmaster was also very cold. Dad suffered another ear bashing on my behalf, duly passed on.

By now, my father had enrolled in the A.R.P as a Warden and mum had joined the W.V S – Womens Voluntary Service. In this capacity she was appointed 'Marshal' for the 3 cellar shelters. Something like a trouble-shooter I guess.

Urgent training was taking place on all aspects of Civil Defence. Every evening the school was in use for lectures and demonstrations of fire fighting, first aid, aircraft identification and all the other multitude of emergency situations that could at any moment confront the civilian population.

Although only 10 years old, I was accepted to such lectures with my parents and soon became something of an expert at aircraft identification and fire fighting with a stirrup pump having had plenty of practice with the shelter pump!

There were also the more specialised aspects of the rescue services such as, Gas decontamination squads – Stretcher bearers and heavy rescue workers recruited from the building industry.

Later on, fire watchers became compulsory for all business premises overnight and had to be provided by staff rota. Consequently, virtually everyone was involved in some capacity or another.

A uniform of some sort almost became normality. The dark blue blouse style jacket of the A.R.P. and my mother's rather fetching green skirt and top with a brimmed hat of the W.V.S.
Once the raids started a 'tin hat' would complete the ensemble, either on the head or slung over one shoulder as the occasion demanded.

Dad came staggering home with a huge bundle of sand-bags.
"What about sand?" said mum. "Couldn't get enough in my pockets" came the flippant reply. "We will have to use soil".
We set to, digging up the lawn, but found even more soil next door. The suspect German – he of the sore head – had disappeared.
Rumour was, that he had been interned for the duration so we reckoned that his back garden now represented captured territory!

Okay, so what do we do with 50 sandbags? The area around the Paraffin oil store seemed to be the best bet, but stacking them was hardly worth all the effort.
It looked rather pathetic to see a completed wall only 5 bags high.

Mum threw a major 'wobbly' after the first rainfall. Soggy dribbles of mud oozed from the bags and trickled down the back yard in dirty rivulets.

With constant foot traffic muddy shoe marks appeared all over the house. Not for the first, or last time, dad had to endure some harsh verbals and instruction on the use of a mop!

During August, German aircraft carried out heavy attacks against shipping and convoys in the English Channel. Further raids developed against coastal towns and ports.

On the 14th a massive coastal attack was launched with as we now know, 1000 aircraft taking part. The entire coastline from Plymouth up to the Tyne was bombarded.

The next few days were to prove ominous and a prelude to the storm.
R.A.F airfields throughout Southern England were attacked by a swarm of 500 plus bombers.
We did not realise then of course, but the 'Battle of Britain' had begun.

Whilst the damage was repaired fighter squadrons were in some cases transferred to obscure 'private' airfields. The facilities were basic but they were relatively safe from attack.

Within days another aerial armada penetrated to the outskirts of London and a massive battle for control of the skies over Southern England began in earnest.
A battle that would determine the destiny of this country.

The sirens were now beginning to sound with increasing frequency. In those early days everyone dashed to a shelter on every occasion, which caused a major disruption to everyday life and loss of vital production. Gradually people learned to adopt a more realistic approach and waited until some danger appeared imminent.

In the meantime, the population were still trying to come to terms with the black-out and the unreality of total intense darkness.

It is difficult now to comprehend just how dark it could be on a night with cloud cover. Not the slightest glimmer of reflected light as people with shaded torches and vehicles with only a small slit of light groped their way around.

All the trees, kerbs and other likely obstacles had broad white painted lines sploshed around them, but even so, people still walked into things.

One lady told me that she used to walk to and from work waving a long cane in front of her, as would a visually impaired person.

We heard that on a bend in the road, several cars had driven straight into the nearby river Brent

One of our shelter regulars came in sporting a lovely 'Shiner'. Resisting the obvious comments she insisted that they had forgotten to mark a telephone pole – so she did!

Some people were still careless with black-out blinds or whatever. Persistant offenders who ignored the bellowed shouts of Air Raid Wardens 'Put that ruddy light out' faced a heavy fine.

We heard of one instance locally whereby neighbours, fearful of their own safety, put a brick through the offending window which seemed to solve the problem!

In the early darkness of the winter months, if it was a gloomy afternoon I recall that classroom lessons were abandoned as it was totally impractical to black-out the large and very numerous sash windows around the school buildings. Woe betide anyone who left a light on!

The young pilots of the Spitfires and Hurricanes, who were to become famed as 'The Few', defended with magnificent courage in almost continuous action that deprived them of the opportunities for rest or relaxation. Called from bed at dawn they sprawled in deckchairs around the dispersal hut until startled by a clanging bell and the cry 'Squadron Scramble!'

At the onset of the 'Battle of Britain', Germany had a numerical advantage of more than 3 to 1 in terms of aircraft.

Figures do tend to vary according to dates but taking a round figure average suggests that they had 1800 bombers and 1500 fighter 'planes. Opposed to this might, The R.A.F were able to muster 750 Spitfires and Hurricanes, plus other inferior aircraft up to a maximum of 900.

Not all aircraft on either side were readily available to the main area of conflict.

The Germans had another great advantage in that many aircrew had battle experience gained during the Spanish civil war, when pilots were sent on rotation to join the 'Condor Legion' operating on the side of General Franco's Nationalist forces.

Also, by the time that raids commenced on Britain, many aircrew had taken part in the initial invasion of Poland and subsequently the Low Countries and France.

For many of the R.A.F pilots it was 'In at the deep end' from day one.

During the initial daylight attacks we often had prior warning that the sirens were about to sound when the Spitfires took off from Northolt and roared up over Greenford and Ealing. With their distinctive Merlin engines at full boost they climbed rapidly to gain maximum height before encountering the incoming hordes somewhere over the Southern counties.

Although we did not know it at the time, the tremendous advantage of Radar determined that most of the aerial battles took place over Southern England and before the raiders could reach London. Sometimes however, they encroached within our sight and we would watch fascinated as white con' – condensation – trails weaved seemingly lazy intricate patterns of swirls and circles high in the blue summer sky.

It was difficult to comprehend that such delicate tracery was being formed by young men pushing their aircraft to extreme in a desperate fight, not only for personal survival, but that of the nation.

We all thrilled to the daily score of enemy aircraft shot down, in much the way that one would follow a cricket scoreboard. We now know that in the heat and confusion of battle some figures were inflated, but at the time we were so excited that our lads were knocking hell out of their lot.

In those early days, not everyone had completed shelter arrangements. The authorities advised that the next best thing was to shelter under the stairs, considered to be the strongest area of the house. However, as today, they were invariably crammed with junk, quite apart from the gas and electricity meters.

I recently met a lady who recalled that when a little girl, her Grandma' was staying with them. The sirens went during the night and as the cupboard still hadn't been cleared, they actually sat on the stairs – probably the least safest place!

Getting out of a nice warm bed it was so cold sitting there that this young girl said "I'm freezing. My teeth are chattering, are your's Nan?"

"Dunno love, mine are upstairs in a glass" came the reply.

The London sirens were now sounding quite often by day and night. With the first night alerts we all leapt out of bed and dashed down to the shelter, but nothing much happened except for distant gunfire and the odd probing searchlight in the far night sky. After a few such occasions my parents became fed up with deserting a warm bed and decided that in future we would all stay put to rely on my young acute ears to give due warning.

The call would come "Roy, are you awake?" "Okay mum, I'm all ears". Days and nights passed without incident. If the All-clear did not sound for a while it was very difficult not to nod off to sleep again. All these interruptions were upsetting our sleep pattern.

History records that many in the German High Command were convinced that London should be the primary target for sustained attack, thereby causing a breakdown of morale among the civilian population and pressure on the government to capitulate.

On the night of August 24th, bombs were dropped within the confines of the Capital, but it is now known that this was by navigational error.

This action provoked a reprisal raid on Berlin by the R.A.F. Hitler was furious, having constantly assured the German people that not one single bomb would ever fall on the Capital city. He promptly gave the Luftwaffe chief Hermann Goering a free hand.

This proved to be a very timely and critical decision. The Luftwaffe immediately ended their ferocious attacks on R.A.F airfields which had proved so devastating to Fighter Command in terms of aircraft losses, being already at full stretch in aerial combat.

History records that the change of policy to concentrate on London proved to be an incalculable error and a turning point, not only in the immediate battle, but to Hitlers planned invasion.

On Saturday September 7th, the sirens sounded in late afternoon. Customers carried on shopping, no-one was particularly worried.

Imperceptably at first, I heard the distant sound of massed aero engines and the thud of anti-aircraft fire. Calling my parents we dashed upstairs to look out over London from the top window. By now there could be no mistaking the ever increasing pulsating throb of German aircraft. A sound that was to become so familiar in the days and nights to come.

The 'ack-ack' guns were now fully in action and our sightseeing ended abruptly. This was for real!

Scampering down the 48 stairs to the cellar we listened with bated breath to the distant 'Crumps' creeping ever closer. Our shelter population increased rapidly as customers and passers-by made a frantic dash to this sanctuary.

Post war records indicate that 1000 enemy aircraft of all types were hurled into this attack. The formations were 1½ miles high and covered 800 square miles of sky in several waves. The onslought was concentrated on the East End and London docks. Most aircraft that passed over West London had already unloaded their deadly cargo.

The 'All-clear' did not sound until 4am in the morning, to invoke a deathly hush appropriate to a Sunday morning. The unbroken discordant whine of Dorniers and the drone of Heinkels, interposed with a cacophony of gunfire and the distant thud of exploding bombs left a hollow pocket in its wake. We were so tired and exhausted by nervous apprehension, like a punch drunk boxer reeling on the ropes. As London grasped blessed relief, little did we know how very brief that respite would prove to be.

That night was in fact the prelude to the 'Blitz' that was to last for 9 long months of traumatic nights.

The following day Goering is quoted as saying 'Adolph Hitler has entrusted me with the task of attacking the heart of the British Empire. From where I stand on the French coast I can see waves of 'planes heading for England and London, which will be totally destroyed'.

That day had been relatively quiet. It must have been late afternoon when Goering spoke. The sirens sounded about 4pm.

The much vaunted anti-aircraft defences certainly made a lot of noise and kept our spirits up with the thoughts that we were fighting back, but subsequent research suggests that they were virtually useless at that time. The sound detectors that accompanied the guns were rendered unreliable by the Luftwaffe method of de-synchronising the twin engines. They were only effective up to 15.000 feet, the German aircraft flew higher. We now know that when the 'Blitz' started, there were only 92 guns in and around London, but they were unable to fire with any accuracy.

Subsequent orders were issued to fire at random, rather like a peashooter aiming at gnats in the dark!

These are not my calculations of course, but something I picked up from an interesting study paper on the subject.

Scientific facts are, that in one cubic mile of airspace there are 5.500.000 cubic yards of air. The lethal impact zone of a shell burst is a mere few thousand yards for a fraction of a second. 'Pot luck' would therefore require a firing rate of 3000 shells to achieve a remote chance of hitting anything!

Having said all that, I did in fact witness a German bomber shot down by ground fire which is described in later pages.

They came again the next night and every night with increasing ferocity. We moved into the cellar shelter with more purpose. Bedclothes were fitted to the double tier bunks and bits of curtain hung to provide a modicum of privacy.

At that time we had not adapted to such a nocturnal existance, lack of sleep and the tension of fear. People had a 'Zombie' like appearance, but displayed a quiet determination to carry on as usual, be it work or school. Life must go on, but for how long we pondered.

West London generally had been fortunate so far, but any doubt or lingering hope that a full scale 'Blitzkrieg' as the Germans called saturation bombing, may not be launched was well and truly dispelled towards the end of September. Night after night, from early evening to the dawn, history records that waves of up to 800 aircraft rained bombs indiscriminately over the capital and few areas escaped this onslought.

Initially, we huddled frightened in the cellar as this cavalcade of death droned overhead. Our shelter filled rapidly with 'Regulars' but was now becoming overcrowded by newcomers, running the gauntlet and breathlessly gasping "Any room down there?" Somehow my parents would find another corner and chair.

Every night the sky was aglow with a cauldron of fire, diffused by the glare of magnesium flares dropped by Luftwaffe 'marker' 'planes to guide in the next wave of bombers.

It is difficult now, to convey the constant feeling of terror and apprehension that everyone felt in those early stages, relieved only by intermittent welcome snatches of sleep.

Incredibly however, we gradually got used to it all and a revised pattern of life developed to accommodate daily duties, school attendance and for the 'Grown-up's' their work or other obligations. A new interpretation of normality

We soon learnt that if flares were being released in our vicinity it was a time to start worrying!

During those first long sleepless nights I experienced the full horror of warfare, being allowed a quick glance out of the shelter doorway during any respite to see the multi-coloured flickering conflagration all around the skyline.

It is strange really, but I do not recall being frightened. Perhaps the sudden awful reality was too much for a young lad to comprehend midst all the excitement, should that be the descriptive word.

Every night the noise seemed to get louder and nearer. Eventually we felt for the first time the earth trembling shudder of nearby high explosive bombs. As we listened with bated breath an aircraft seemed to pass directly overhead and we heard a successive rushing whistle as a stick of bombs was released to hurtle earthward and shattering oblivion.

Instinctively, we all grovelled on the cellar floor until the distant explosions, then rather sheepishly regained composure as someone said "This is bloody dangerous!"

In fact, we soon learned that such sounds could be very deceptive. The bombs landed far away but could well have passed over our heads.

All the so called 'experts' in our shelter reckoned, 'It's the one's you don't hear you have to worry about'. That intrigued me. Surely, if you didn't hear it you wouldn't worry anyway.

Every morning we emerged bleary eyed into the dawn expecting to see some damage, but so far our locality remained intact. There was however, a virtually permanent pall of black smoke suspended like a blanket over the London skyline and the air was tainted with an acrid smell of burning.

We would climb the stairs to our vantage point at the top of the house to gaze in awe at the shroud which covered the city, interposed with pockets of pulsating fire erupting skyward as buildings collapsed. We would stand in silence, trying to imagine the awful destruction that must exist. One morning we glimpsed a great consolation. As early morning sunshine penetrated the haze, just for a moment the cross on the dome of St Pauls Cathedral glistened. At least that symbol was intact and destined to remain so throughout the 'Blitz'. An oasis of faith in a desert of destruction.

Despite being shattered by the ongoing nightly events, most kids went to school as usual. On the way we would search for anti-aircraft shell shrapnel in the streets. None of us found anything at that stage. A few bits of rusty metal produced by one lad received the derision it deserved from us 'know-alls'. It was the general opinion that despite the severity of the attacks the Western suburbs had still escaped lightly. For how much longer we wondered.

We were now becoming that much better equipped, both mentally and materially for the coming nights. As dusk fell our cellar shelterers would arrive clutching bags of sandwiches and Thermos flasks. Also personal comforts conducive to a more permanent residence that was to last for more than a year, although at that time no-one had any idea of the eventual duration. Just as well! Virtually every day, particularly in the early morning or evening the air was tainted by a musty tang of burnt wood and dust. If the weather was inclined to be foggy, smoke from thousands of coal fire chimneys would add to this blanket of pollution.

This nightmare was to last for 57 consecutive nights to November 2nd when a brief spell of bad weather gave a respite, but the 'Blitz' then resumed for another 15 consecutive nights.

Among our shelter regulars, one elderly lady remains indelibly in my mind. I wonder how old she really was? To me then, I reckoned at least 99!

Of rather large proportions, she always wore a voluminous black dress and petrified me with her strident disciplinarian voice. People said that she had been a school headmistress. I suspected that this must have been a borstal!

I dreaded her becoming a long term regular.

"Mum, I can't stand that woman always shouting at me. You're the Marshal, ride her out of town or something. Why not shove her in next doors shelter?"

She insisted that it was her right to enter via our front door. By now, others were happy to use the public entrance from the pavement.

I would answer the doorbell and mumble "'ello". She would boom, "Don't mumble boy. I am Mrs Cheeseman. You say good evening Mrs Cheeseman – Yes Mrs Cheeseman – No Mrs Cheeseman – goodbye Mrs Cheeseman. Do you hear me?"
Oh I did. It was in the right sequence as well!

Actually, she mellowed and developed a 'soft spot' for me.
One day she gave me a large tin of mixed foreign stamps collected by her late husband.
I was astounded. Had someone actually married her!

She also gave me a rather grotty pair of collar studs with the entreaty "Look after them, they are valuable".
Having done so for many years into adulthood, I eventually found them to be quite ordinary and worthless. That does sound ungrateful, but there must be a moral somewhere. I kept them for nigh on 50 years.

Night after night the sirens sounded soon after dusk and the only reaction became 'Bit late tonight' or 'Gor blimey, give us a chance for a bit of tea'. Evening activity was often spasmodic as if they were feeling out the opposition, but it was a sure bet that from mid evening there would be no further respite throughout the night.
Even the weather took on a new significance. Clear frosty nights were dreaded. 'Bombers moon' it was termed.
There were no such things as weather forecasts on the wireless. That would have provided an excellent service to the enemy. Instead, newspapers published charts listing all the possible permutations of weather factors, such as cloud formations, shape and texture, wind

direction and temperature etc, from which one could make a fairly accurate forecast. This became my speciality having got the first few reasonably correct. Shelter guests greeted me "Hi Roy, how's the weather tonight?"

I reckon that our humble efforts were more accurate than some of the modern day forecasts I have heard.

School life was getting very difficult, but as I recall, absence was rare despite such a lack of sleep. It was not uncommon for pupils to nod off at their desk, but such lapses were treated with tolerance and understanding by the teachers who were themselves very tired. Life must go on as normal as possible.

All through September the nightly raids continued unabated, sapping the strength, but not the resolve of Londoners, whose fortitude has passed into the annals of history.

One fine sunny day the Luftwaffe added a new dimension to the attack.

It was not uncommon for the sirens to sound several times during daylight hours, but people learned to adapt. Raids were usually brief and not too alarming, consequently, everyday life carried on.

The shop was busy and I was mucking about in the shed at the end of our back yard. Gradually I became aware of the heavy and quite unmistakable throb of German aircraft engines and the thud of anti-aircraft fire.

Dashing in to warn mother I found that everyone was already aware and standing out on the pavement gazing towards London.

As the thunder increased in volume and the aircraft came into view we were transfixed by an incredible sight as waves of bombers swept over in well drilled formations, seemingly untroubled by desultory shell bursts.

There was a mad stampede to our cellar shelter but no bombs fell in our area. Post war German records indicate that 450 aircraft were involved. Historical analysts conclude that on this occasion our defences misinterpreted the objective.

It was thought that heading for London in daylight was a feint and the real targets would prove to be a renewed attack on R.A.F airfields. Consequently, in an effort to outsmart the enemy our fighters were 'sectored' to what proved to be the wrong areas.

This raid had a detrimental effect to morale for a while. Not so much the damage, again to the long suffering East End, but the fact that they were able to fly over virtually in review order.

We did not know the circumstances at the time and it was some consolation to learn later that many German aircraft had been shot down on the return leg to France as the re-deployed fighter squadrons caught up with them.

Whether a direct result of this episode one will never know, but we received what we felt to be our own personal protection. Everyone was excited that a battery of eight heavy anti-aircraft guns were being installed in our local Gunnersbury Park – an apt name really!

We walked up to have a look, but the park was shut and patrolled by armed guards. However, we were able to sneak a view through an obscure side gate to see the long menacing barrels pointing skyward from earth and sandbag temporary emplacements.

Later, these became permanent concrete sites with interconnecting roads.

That night the racket was incredible. No chance of sleep now!

There could be no doubt that many more guns had been moved into London. The raiders certainly had a hot reception that night as the air was filled with a cacophony of perpetual noise. The guns in our local park punched the ears like a boxer's glove and made the cellar floor tremble. Whether they actually hit anything is another matter, but it certainly cheered us all up. Indeed, there was an air of excitement that we were at last fighting back with some venom. To hell with sleep, let's enjoy the pandemonium!

Dad called me to the front entrance of the shelter to hear the shrapnel pattering down like hail as it sparkled off the roofs or into the road, bringing with it broken roof slates to add to the general racket.

Great stuff, there must be plenty of souvenirs in the morning. As we turned to go back down the steps, prompted by a yell from mum, something about irresponsible fathers, a large piece clanged onto the pavement just outside the entrance. Dad moved with some speed, but I suspect that this was mums vocal motivation!

Why do I remember all the little things so well? Sitting round the open range kitchen fire in the early evenings, toasting slices of bread on the end of a long wire toasting fork made by brother Bern. There was not enough butter to afford the luxury of melting this over toast, but good old mum could always be relied upon to come up with a scraping of dripping fat, or even marrow jam. Delicious, I can almost taste it now.

Once a week, Friday as I remember, we would have a special treat for tea. Scrambled egg on toast. Not real eggs, but the powdered version. Whipped up it was fine, but if say an omelette was attempted, the end result could also be used to sole a shoe!

Despite the obvious dangers, my father, sister, and her husband Arthur preferred to sleep upstairs in the kitchen. As mum always said "Your dad could sleep on a clothes line". He was happy to settle in his armchair, whilst Ivy and Arthur shared a mattress on top of a large blanket box as they were called. Indeed, I still have this box in use.

Medically unfit for military service, Arthur joined the Auxiliary Fire Service and eventually served on a River Thames 'Firefloat' in the thick of the action around the London Docks. I can so readily recall the acrid pungent smell of smoke that wafted around the house whenever he returned home. Filthy dirty, dog tired and often still soaking wet, having returned on the underground train in that condition.

One's sense of smell will often trigger recollection of a person or situation. Perfume is of course, a prime example. For me, the smell of charred wood will always bring back a picture of Arthur trudging wearily in the hallway, helmet in hand, to lightly punch me in the ribs and say "Hi Buster – How's tricks?"

Normal night attire was totally impractical with the ever present contingency of an emergency. Inhibitions were therefore discarded as men merely slipped out of their trousers and ladies their skirt or slacks. A popular innovation was the 'Siren suit', similar to the present day tracksuit. They were ideal to withstand the rigours of constantly flopping around. Sensibility was the keynote of what little remained as dress sense.

Bombs were now beginning to fall alarmingly close and the law of averages began to crop up in pessimistic conversations. One of the first really heavy one's to fall in our vicinity struck just 300 yards away in a wide alley type access road behind the next parade of shops, but separated by a side road. There was an almighty thud and the floor of the cellar trembled as we felt for the first time that vacuum in the ears that signified a 'near one'. Daylight revealed a massive crater. The bomb had buried deeply in the soft earth before exploding. It tore out a hole, big enough as they all said, 'to put a couple of double-decker buses in'. Despite being cushioned by the depth of the explosion and the combined width of the alley and gardens, blast damage was destructive. Scarcely a window remained over a 100 yard radius and many roofs were stripped naked of slates.

In total contrast, a few nights later a bomb of reputedly the same calibre fell almost parallel in line two streets away. This struck the dead centre of the road and again ripped out a huge crater that encroached into the front gardens either side, but scarcely a pane of glass was broken!

This gave rise to an assumption that it did not explode, known as a UXB. The area was cordoned off with tapes and the houses evacuated. This was only a 100 yards from our school gate and next morning our way was barred by an elderly copper, "Can't go down there, it's a UXB".

From a distance we gazed at this abyss and commented "Cor, with that ruddy great 'ole, good job it didn't go orf ain' it?" It was not long before the bomb disposal squad arrived and immediately took down the cordons, despite our fervent objections for this meant that we had to go to school tomorrow!

Talking to the army lads, the conclusion was that the blast had somehow gone straight up into the air. It certainly had a strange effect sometimes. Local archive records still designate this as a UXB.

Incredibly, even the gardens on the very edge of the crater were virtually undisturbed, except that one elderly lady who was a regular shop customer was complaining bitterly that she had lost a row of newly planted vegetables and could not get to her front door.

Before the war dad had dabbled with painting and decorating and this particular widowed lady always insisted that her house frontage be painted every second year, with exactly the same manufacture and shade of pale green paint, despite entreaties to have a change. This ritual continued after the war and when I recently passed the house after a lapse of some 60 years I was astonished to see it still the same colour. Surely it is not the same lady. Must be 130 years old by now! Let's conclude that dad made a good job of the painting.

It was about this time that we had a real life spy drama by way of diversion. My sister had occasion to nip up to her bedroom at the back of the house whilst German aircraft were around. As she paused to glance out of the window at the searchlights and bursting flak in the sky, a coloured flashing light caught her eye. This seemed to come from the vicinity of a row of houses about 500 yards away on the other side of the underground railway cutting which ran close by. It was very difficult to judge distance in the total darkness, diffused by the gun flashes and searchlights. With everything blacked-out, a flashing light would have to be deliberate. She waited, then, simultaneous with another aircraft overhead, came another series of flashes. That's it! there could be no mistake. Ivy dashed excitedly down to the cellar to gabble her findings to the police officer who 'hid' in the shelter when things got a bit hot outside.

Nothing further occurred that night and my sister became very upset at all the insinuations. "Are you sure? Probably a reflection of searchlights" or "It was the ack-ack" and so on. Plus of course the odd whispered "Silly cow".

Next morning a couple of army officers arrived together with Police. Mum said "What has that silly girl started now".

Obviously, in daylight nothing could be done. Visually it could have come from any of a row of houses, or even a taller building further away. It would have to involve a night vigil and the officers settled themselves into the top back room.

We were all sworn to secrecy and although 'busting to tell' I was made to solemnly promise not to mention this at school.

It seemed quite incredulous to me that the officers asked to borrow my binoculars, which were not very good and also had a loose lens that fell out at the slightest provocation. Surely the army was not in that state!

As a potential spy drama this was falling well short of my expectations.

It could now be taken for granted that there would be a raid that night. This had become such a ritual that the only question was, what time would it start. The intrepid spy catchers settled down with tea flasks and sandwiches. They were happy with such a good 'scrounge' in homely comfort.

The first night, as the familiar throb of aero engines gathered in the night sky from mid-evening, seemed hopeful.

An aircraft seemed to be circling at a lower altitude as searchlights groped to pick it up. Could this be it?

Perhaps it was neither the time or place for a young lad, but I was not going to miss this. Anyway, they were my binoculars!

My mother was understandably agitated. Fair enough, the raid had every indication of being a heavy one by the sound of things and we were right at the top of the house.

Suddenly, to a collective exclamation, there it was! An unmistakable flashing light that came at intermittant intervals. Just had to be code of some sort.

Ivy yelled "Told you so!". Various people made a grab at the binoculars, the lens fell out and chaos reigned in the darkness with people groping around the floor to find it, midst shouting and arguing.

Everyone peered intently into the darkness trying to pinpoint the exact location, but it was impossible to do so with any accuracy. The light continued to flash and no doubt remained that this synchronised with the arrival of aircraft.

By now, the officers were in a state of frustrated confusion. Ideas were being bandied about and rejected as impractical. Until something ridiculously simple occured to me.

"Er, excuse me, I have an idea". "Not now lad, we are busy"

The chaos continued, so did the light. Try again. "Scuse me"

"Not now son, we are too busy" – Could have fooled me!

They were not going to get rid of me that easily and I persisted until in desperation one of the officers said "Okay, lets have it, then get down to the shelter".

What rubbish was to come from this lad who shouldn't be around anyway.

"Why not bang two nails into the window sill in line with the light, then knock the heads down until the angle is okay. All we need to do in daylight is to look along them and there you are".

Silence for a few moments. I waited for someone to say "I was just going to say that", then a flurry of activity to find a hammer and thin nails. Needless to say, mum knew exactly where to find them.

After all the dithering about, it was no surprise that in the meantime the raid quietened down and the light was not seen again that night. Never mind, there is always tomorrow.

The army lads were quite happy to return. Mum was spoiling them with home comforts far removed from barrack life.

Came the night. The sirens sounded. Hammer, nails, taped up lens, but no light! Nor indeed the following night and a week elapsed with increasing frustration. Interest began to wane and all concerned were getting rather fed up with the whole affair. Ivy was in dire danger of being maligned once again.

One significant feature had become obvious, that no enemy aircraft had flown low in the vicinity, despite successive heavy raids. Finally, on the seventh and what was to be the final night of 'spywatch', they were alerted by the increasing volume of a distinctive whoom-whoom drone of a prowling aircraft.

To frantic exclamations and activity, the light began to flash. The hammer and nails were put to good effect and they even had time to finely adjust the angles until accuracy was assured.

At first light next morning the skylight of a terraced house some quarter of a mile away was perfectly pinpointed. This was well adrift of even the best previous guess.

We never really knew what happened after that. The officers dashed off and a senior police officer visited mum and dad. A security ban clamped down and we were all warned to uphold total secrecy. Almost impossible for me as an impressionable young lad, but I did manage it.

We did hear later whispers that when the house was raided, the bird had flown. Rather ironical bearing in mind that a week had been wasted. I was not impressed. I had a personal interest in this fellow and reckoned that he should have been 'nailed'.

School lessons were becoming a very erratic affair. Whilst daylight raids were limited, there were nuisance attacks. Generally carried out by small formations of faster fighter-bombers to keep everyone on their toes and cause continual disruption.

This meant that the sirens sounded several times a day and much of our time was being spent down the playground shelters, where initially we just sang or chatted. Then some silly teacher had the bright idea that we should actually try to learn something. Stupid woman, didn't she know that there was a war on?

Actually, it was not too bad. Normal lessons were impractical, but general knowledge quizzes, word games and number puzzles were devised that were quite good fun to while away the time as we sat around the tunnel-like shelters, dimly lit by Hurricane oil lamps.

After school hours I helped dad to shut all the windows around the three buildings, check that no water taps, or importantly, lights had been left on. There was always time for me to kick a ball around the playground before going home and I suppose it had to happen. Crash! Straight through the head-mistresses study window went the tennis ball, leaving a rather neat round hole.

"Oh gawd" now I was in trouble! Dad was not impressed. However, as I explained to him, it was not really a problem. The hole wasn't actually caused by a ball, it was shrapnel. All he had to do next morning was to knock out some more pieces, I would give him a lump of shrapnel to place on the floor – end of story. Hitler would get the blame and we would be off the hook.

Ah well, the best laid plans. Fate was to decree otherwise.

That night, dad was on firewatch duty at the school. Being so young and naive and despite all the frivolous and snide comments, it never occurred to me how very compromising such arrangements must have been. Male and female staff shared the long night vigil. I can now imagine what devious plans must have been made to partner the young fanciable music teacher for instance.

One can only conclude that there must have been occasions in various establishments when 'Nero fiddled whilst Rome burned!'

Anyway, dad's luck was right out. On September 30th 1940 he was on duty paired up with the very prim and proper headmistress of the junior school. I can only recount their graphic description of the nights events.

They had been dozing in armchairs in the senior school staff room until the sirens sounded. This room had been adapted for fire-watch duties by the provision of a bunk bed and tea making facilities. I wonder now, how did anyone ever get a decent nights sleep in those days?

It was around midnight when they heard a 'Whooshing' noise, totally unlike the conventional whistle of a high explosive bomb, or the softer whisper of incendiaries. This was followed by a deep thud that reverberated through the building but without obvious explosion.

The following silence was uncanny. Surely, this could only be a UXB. but as dad said "Something was not quite right".

With a great deal of trepidation the valiant pair set out with only a shaded torch to aid their search throughout the considerable expanse of three buildings and playgrounds, fearing that any moment they would confront a gaping hole in floor or ceiling.

Almost immediately they became aware of a pungent smell that became stronger and more irritating by the minute. Their eyes began to smart and for a moment, gas was the awful thought, but logic prevailed. The effects would have been far more decisive than an obnoxious smell and some minor discomfort.

They groped their way through the senior and junior buildings – Nothing. The quest was taking a long time. Where was this 'thing' whatever it may be. Although, as they subsequently confessed, they were afraid to find it anyway! One masked torch was not helpful.

Just the infants section to go now. Dad opened the connecting gate between the playgrounds and stepped through. Straight into a noxious evil smelling 'Goo' that was adhering to everything like a clinging sticky blanket. Floundering back in some confusion, it was impossible to determine either what it was, or the extent of the situation.

Enemy aircraft were still overhead and the torch could only be used with great care, but enough to see that the substance was black, thick, sticky and smelt awful.

They made their way round to the front street entrance to the playground which appeared to be clear and carefully stepped forward. Pace by pace, half way now. The smell was sickening, then suddenly, 'Slurp' under the sole of dad's shoe. There was the tidemark. Whatever it was covered about half the large playground.

Notifying the local wardens post of an incident, all were mystified, but nothing could be done until daylight would reveal exactly what they would have to deal with.

First reactions in the cold light of day were "What a helluva mess!" Everything in sight was covered by this stinking black gunge. The fire services were very cautious and called in an expert to verify that this was a little used incendiary device, known as an oil bomb. The canister had skidded down the side wall of the caretaker's house tearing out a deep groove in the brickwork. The drum had either then burst with the force of impact, or more likely, had exploded, as great chunks of the container had sliced into surrounding woodwork, particularly the playground rain shelter.

THE SCHOOL CARETAKERS HOUSE TODAY. ARROWS DEPICT WHERE THE OIL BOMB SKIDDED DOWN THE WALL. THE PLAYGROUND RAIN SHELTER IS TO THE RIGHT OF THIS PICTURE.

THE ONLY REMAINING RAIN SHELTER BEAM BEARING A SCAR OF IMPACT. OTHER BEAMS HAVE BEEN REPLACED OVER THE YEARS.

Fortunately, the incendiary ignition must have failed, leaving the treacle like morass inert and relatively safe. Once again, by an incredible quirk, not one pane of glass had been broken, yet several pieces of metal were embedded into a door and classroom window frames.

Poor dad! As caretaker he was responsible for keeping the playgrounds clean and tidy. Ribald comments came thick and fast about the state of this one! Seriously, it was a massive problem how to get rid of this stuff. Someone even suggested putting a match to it!

The fire service arranged for a couple of lorry loads of sand to be spread, which slowly soaked up the oil. It took at least 2 weeks of hard graft before the playground could be used again.

For many years I kept the filler cap of this device which dad found among the oil, together with pieces of the casing prised out of the woodwork. In view of the current interest in memorabilia it is a pity that my impressive collection was thrown away when I married and moved home.

For many years as I drove home from work at Maidenhead, I instinctively glanced at the wall of the caretaker's house. The score mark was clearly visible for some 30 years until one day I was disappointed to see workmen renovating the pebbledash and finally obliterating the last poignant reminder of that incident.

I had occasion to attend a football meeting at the school nigh on 40 years after the war. I was able to show my colleagues the gouged woodwork under the rain shelter. The deeply scarred timber seemed so familiar and certainly bridged the passage of time. Later that evening I stood alone for a while and felt very close to dad. Perhaps I was. The picture of him was clear enough, laboriously sweeping and shovelling that mucky gunge day after day.

Oh yes! What happened about the broken window? Dad forgot all about it. The headmistress had a go about allowing ball games after hours and he had to repair it in his lunch hour. Why was I not popular?

Some of the anti-aircraft guns now brought in were mounted on lorries for mobility. These were the multi barrelled 'Bofors' capable of a rapid rate of fire at 80 rounds of 40mm shells per minute. One evening we were all sitting around the cellar chatting, when the sound of a heavy vehicle could be heard up in the street.

What was going on? Shouting could now be heard. Urged on, dad cautiously climbed the wooden steps to carefully lift the metal cover at pavement level. At precisely the wrong moment!

No sooner had he discerned a vehicle parked directly outside, then simultaneously with the shouted command FIRE!, the multiple barrels spit fire with a rapid succession of Bang –bang-bang as it hurled shells skyward.

Down the cellar we all jumped 'out of our skins', but dad was so startled that the metal lid slammed down on his fingers as he tumbled back down the steps yelling something about flippin' fingers. Fortunately his pride was hurt more than body, apart from sore fingers. Devoid of much sympathy one of the men commented 'Always said you should get your finger out'.

After the initial burst of fire the vehicle moved off. Maybe it was on its way to an open location, saw a target and could not resist 'aving a pop.

I recently had the priviledge of chatting to a very sprightly young man of 94 who lived in our locality and knew my parents. He was in the Home Guard – 'Dad's Army' right from its formation and eventually rose to the rank of Lieutenant.

He told me of an incident that occurred just a couple of streets away from our shop.

At this early stage of the war weapons of any sort were in short supply, but on the day in question they were thrilled to receive old rifles, possibly of World War 1 vintage, together with 10 rounds of ammunition. All were smothered in thick solid grease.

Without an Anderson shelter, his father had converted their downstairs lounge into a strengthened gas proof area with timber supports and sealing tape around all the windows.

His sister was a seamstress and with 'Make do and mend' a priority her talents were in demand. She used a spare upstairs back room as a work place, with sewing machine and ironing board etc.

The sirens sounded and the family gathered in the 'Safe' room. As occupational therapy it seemed a good idea to make a start on cleaning off the grease.

Suddenly, from somewhere upstairs came a solid thud. They looked at each other wonderingly. "What the hell was that?"

Opening the door to investigate he was confronted by the extraordinary sight of their cat going absolutely berserk, literally racing from one end of the hall to the other and climbing the walls in obvious terror.

As he said "Just like a Tom and Jerry cartoon".

He opened the front door and the moggy shot out like the proverbial scalded cat. Still bemused and muttering something like 'That animal will have to go. He is madder than the rest of us", he shut the door and turned back to look up the stairs. Don't panic! – flames were licking round the open door of his sisters workroom.

Chucking buckets of water had little effect at that stage. It was now obvious that an incendiary bomb had come through the roof and the magnesium globules were merely re-igniting after an initial deluge. They rang the fire service and with the help of neighbours who formed a bucket chain the fire was eventually confined to that room.

Surveying the damage it was obvious that the device had come through the roof, loft area and ceiling, rapidly burnt a very neat round hole through the ironing board, then lodged in the floorboards.

So what had upset the cat? They immediately realised that the invariably warm ironing board was his favourite snoozing place!

He must have been there when the bomb came through the roof, but it will never be known whether he moved quick enough before it actually struck the ironing board.

Either way, it must have been one helluva alarm call!

I reckon that we would all be climbing up the wall in such circumstances.

The cat did return home but never again slept upstairs.

I often wonder how, or indeed if, the modern housewife would cope with the time and ritual involved with my mother's Monday washing day.

'Please don't rain' always the fervent plea.

Initially, the collars and cuffs of shirts and the like, would be hand scrubbed on a corrugated zinc lined washboard.

These things had a new lease of life in the 50s when Lonnie Donnegan made 'Skiffle' popular with the youngsters.

Aspiring lads drummed out so called tunes with thimble covered fingers on them, whilst others strummed on a taut string secured to the middle of an upturned plywood tea chest.

Anyway, with the scrubbing stage complete the clothes would then be dunked into the copper, boiling and bubbling away like a witches cauldron in a corner of the scullery.

With soap strictly rationed, a sparse shake of soap flakes or shavings had to suffice.

The ensuing mass was then poked, prodded and stirred with a wooden copper stick in a haze of steam.

The stick was bleached to a pale fibrous hue by many years usage.

The wash completed, garments were then put through the mangle.

A spring loaded wooden roller contraption hand turned by a large wheel. This squeezed out most of the surplus water. Just a bit slower than the spin dryers of today.

Monday was always associated with a dank steamy atmosphere that seemed to pervade the entire house.

Rituals completed, the clothes were then hung out to dry on the back yard clothes line.

I well remember one occasion after a daylight raid that mum came in 'hopping mad'. A piece of shrapnel had gashed a rip in her pink 'bloomers'!

How times change. When I returned to my old home for a nostalgic visit and to gain some atmosphere for penning these chapters, I was disorientated. The house and shop area has been incorporated with the next door premises. Walls had new doorways, others had been knocked down and corridors installed. Where was I?

Gradually it made sense.

The scullery is now part of an office and a computer stands where the copper used to be. My bedroom is also an office and has a rear entrance staircase down to the back yard now concreted over as a car park. However, from the top of the house one can still enjoy a panoramic view over London, albeit obscured by many new tall buildings.

At the same time I took the opportunity to look around Little Ealing schools. This has now been modified for use as a pre-school centre and primary school only. Obviously, many changes have taken place over the years, but basically the buildings retain their structure and character.

It was very interesting to wander around and recognise so many familiar features, all of which brought back memories.

A children's play area with climbing frames on a safety surface now covers the site of the underground shelters.

Arthur had some terrible tales to tell of his experiences on the Thames Firefloat.

It was somewhere around the East India Dock that the intense heat from burning warehouses blistered the paintwork of the vessel.

On windy nights blazing embers whirled away to start fresh fires elsewhere.

The packed warehouses spilled highly inflammable materials such as rum, sugar and rubber etc, to run as molten rivers along adjoining streets. He told us about a store of raw sugar that collapsed on the waterside, sending a fiery mass of molten 'goo' cascading onto the water surface and flowing towards their boat. I am sure that at times Arthur fervently wished that he was fit enough to join the forces!

By now, it was not only London that was taking a battering. The populations of other ports and cities were suffering. Coventry was subjected to a night of such annihilating ferocity that the Germans coined a new phrase – Coventrieren, to Coventrate.

It was still the East End of London that suffered most. In the early days many people fled every night to makeshift camp sites in Epping Forest. Others sheltered in the Chislehurst caves, ancient Limestone mines, South East of London. In due course these accommodated 15.000 people. As occupational therapy the craftsmen among them constructed a hospital, library, canteen and even a concert hall.

One of the biggest shelters was in Stepney, where up to 16.000 people huddled together midst filthy conditions in a subterranean goods yard.

London underground stations were invaded by huge crowds seeking safety. However, these were not as safe as people imagined. At the time it was hushed up, but post war records reveal that over 100 were killed when a bomb penetrated the tunnel roof before exploding at Bank station.

My parents were always on the look out for something to sell in place of the usual commodities now in short supply. Dad found some unusual items such as luminous discs to wear on coat lapels in the black-out and a new fangled luminous paint that could be daubed on doorbells and gate latches. This was a novelty and splashed around with some enthusiasm.

About this time the colour on top of pillar boxes was changed from the familiar red to a drab yellow. This would change back to red in the event of a gas attack. Rather disconcerting if one was about to post a letter!

Still flushed with success regarding the spy episode, sister Ivy unwittingly created a 'panic stations' situation a few weeks later. Again she had reason to nip upstairs to her bedroom during an evening raid, as always, sneaking a glance out of the window to see what was going on outside. Peering into the night sky illuminated by anti-aircraft gunfire and the glare of searchlights her eye caught something. 'What's that' she mused, as a white circle became visible high in the sky. Simultaneously, an inquisitive searchlight swung over to illuminate a parachute, then another and another.

"Oh my God, it's happening – it's the invasion" she cried.

Her yelling and shouting brought mum and future sister-in-law Joyce running to watch as those parachutes descended about a mile away to the West. With the ever present threat of invasion uppermost in everyone's mind, it just did not occur to them that this could be the crew of a stricken aircraft baling out.

Instead, they reduced the shelter occupants to a state of abject terror and impending doom. A deathly hush descended as twenty or so people sat sweating with apprehension, listening intently for the pealing of church bells, the official signal for an invasion, or perhaps the sound of ground-fire in the streets. No-one was brave enough to poke their head out!

The minutes ticked by. All remained quiet. Even the raid petered out and the All-clear sounded, which was unusual for late evening.

The congregation remained mystified until dad breezed in from his Wardens duties. "Evening all. Saw the guns get one of the buggers earlier on. The crew baled out and they reckon that the Home Guard lads picked 'em up over Boston Manor way".

What a relief! Everyone laughed and joked nervously as they confessed to being scared stiff.

Sister Ivy slunk away quietly muttering "Must keep my big mouth shut".

Normality was restored when the sirens sounded again about midnight to signify that this was to be a two phase raid. Now we could settle down for some much needed sleep!

Mum had the last word – as usual! "That's it. That girl is not going upstairs again during a raid. It's far too worrying for the rest of us". Then, as an afterthought, "Wonder who was lucky enough to get the parachute silk?". Some local ladies would be wearing silk knickers in due course.

The following photograph illustrates the present day scenario of my parents shop. The style and facia are much changed beneath the name of Levy. The original next door hairdressers has been incorporated into the one establishment. Similarly, the adjacent confectioners is now an integral part of the bank.

The heavy metal covers that protected the shelter entrance are still embedded into the pavement.

The current occupier now uses the cellar for storage purposes and was fascinated when I was able to describe the wartime function. He had always been intrigued by evident new brickwork that blocks off the original communicating doors. Also, why the roof timbers were scarred and chunked, which was by the bolts and grapnels supporting the secondary roof.

His conclusion regarding the front metal cover with a large turnscrew plate was, 'It's a coal chute'.

It was a very strange feeling to stand chatting to him in the very space that my trestle bed occupied all those years ago. It was not well lit down there and shadowy images took on a new dimension

A CURRENT VIEW OF MY PARENTS SHOP, THE STYLE AND FASCIA MUCH CHANGED BENEATH THE NAME LEVY.

of bygone faces. I felt a chill as the wooden stairs creaked in a so familiar way.

During the period of the 'Blitz' I walked in my sleep for the one and only time in my life.

The worrying aspect is the sheer blatant exhibitionism. My mother insisted that no matter the circumstances, I had to change into pyjamas at night. To me, this was a real pain when everyone else could flop around as they liked.

The story was subsequently told, that late one evening during the height of a raid and in front of a packed shelter, I slowly arose from my bed, made up from dad's painting trestles, and before this large appreciative audience, proceeded to remove my pyjamas. Wearing only a vacant expression I then walked up the cellar stairs, along the hallway and up the stairs to my bedroom on the first floor. Evidently, mum followed quietly behind and when we reached my bed, gently guided my arm, whispering all the while "Come along Roy, let's sleep in the shelter tonight shall we?".

Obediently I retraced my steps down to the cellar to the undisguised delight of a giggling twelve year old girl peeping out from her bunk. I was totally unaware of this incident until some years later, but it did explain my original consternation when she kept calling me 'Wee Willie Winkie' for no apparent reason.

I wonder if that little girl would recognise me after all these years? Maybe not, I doubt that she would recall my face!

Our row of shops commenced with an off-license, followed by a bank, confectioners, then our hardware store. On the other side was the ladies hairdressers, a cycle shop and the small entrance to South Ealing Underground Station.

On the other side of the railway bridge was a similar block of seven shops at the end of which was a side road. A small church school premises stood on the corner. This had been requisitioned for use as an Auxiliary Fire Station housing a couple of pumps that were towed by vans. It is interesting to note that 3000 London taxis were similarly adapted to haul water pumps.

Opposite our shop was a row of terraced houses.

It was about one-o'clock in the morning that the 'Big one' fell. I was sound asleep until it struck with fearsome force. My first conscious awareness was that my head hurt, presumably having struck the wall at the side of my bed. Also, why was I now lying on the cold stone floor?

In fact, all 16 people in the cellar that night had been heaved out of their bunks or chairs and deposited into a milling heap of confused bodies. With a brick wall at my feet I was left alone in that small section.

Upstairs in the kitchen, Dad, Ivy and Arthur, none of whom were on duty that night, were awake and very aware of the enemy aircraft droning overhead. They said afterwards that a loud unexplainable 'Crack' was distinctly heard, then a brief period of silence until the exploding crescendo of noise and glare like Dante's Inferno as the bomb struck somewhere very close.

Choking masonry dust rolled in through every shattered window as my family recovered from being thrown into a terrified yelling jumble on the floor. Coughing and spluttering in the dark confusion they shouted at each other to counteract the ringing singing deafness in their ears. Fortunately, the window sticky tape and the heavy blanket black-out curtains, although shredded to destruction, had contained the flying glass and none were cut or injured apart from bruising.

Downstairs in the cellar we were fully aware that this one was very close. We must have looked quite a sight. One end of the cellar was partitioned off as a coal store. All the coal dust wafting around added to the dirt and dust filtering down through every crack and crevice. Our ears were popping and painful from the explosive vacuum.

A frantic exchange of shouts with those upstairs verified that everyone was O.K.

I can remember tea and water being passed around to slake throats and nostrils tanged by that peculiar dry sulphuric taste of high explosive. Flannels and hankies soon followed, to wipe away some of the grime from grubby faces.

So, the big question. Where had it struck?

A couple of soldiers had missed the last train and stayed in our shelter, they joined our regular copper and together with dad, Ivy and Arthur, the group ventured outside.

With trembling apprehension they emerged from the shelter entrance into a 'Pea-soup' fog of choking dust to be immediately misled by a red glow from the road opposite. However, this proved to be a single terraced house set ablaze by an incendiary bomb, presumably dropped by the same aircraft. The two soldiers stayed there to see if they could do anything and to ensure that people were not trapped inside.

It was subsequently discovered that the lady of the house was in our cellar, together with her son home on leave from the Navy. He had persuaded her to take shelter. Hitherto, she had cowered under the staircase. The house was completely gutted and both lost everything but the clothes they stood up in.

By now, everyone was saying "Where's the bloody fire brigade". It was unknown then, but the auxiliary fire lads, some of whom were injured, were fighting desperately to extricate themselves from the wrecked school, then, having done so, finding the two vans and pumps little more than mangled heaps of scrap iron.

To my family and friends the direction of the dust cloud wafting over the bridge in the inky blackness of the night provided a clue. Turning past our shopfront they immediately realised the extent of the destruction. Plate glass from the shop windows crunched underfoot and they stumbled over display goods and wreckage strewn all over the road and pavement. Next morning, one of our customers returned a Paraffin oil stove found in her front garden some 100 yards away. Incredibly, a cardboard label entitled E.BARTLETT HARDWARE was still attached by string and the stove was only slightly damaged.

Visibility was slowly improving as they picked their way forward through increasing depths of debris over the bridge.

The facing wall of the shops became discernable in the dark haze, then horrific realisation that nothing more remained. The seven shops had been reduced in an instant to a huge expanse of rubble and wreckage that straddled the road and beyond.

My sister recalled that apart from the perpetual drone of enemy aircraft, which by now had become commonplace to the conscious mind, it was the absolute silence of that desolate scene that invoked a feeling of helpless anguish and horror.

The people beneath that grotesque pile of masonry were close friends and fellow shopkeepers. One infinitesimal factor and the roles could have been reversed. Who knows? Did the German bomb aimer twitch or flinch in that split second as he pushed the release button to determine the destiny of souls below.

The rescue services were now arriving to commence the search for survivors. By next morning, the toll was grim. Ultimately 7 bodies were recovered from the debris, 12 people were injured and 3 members of one family were never found. We knew them all.

The cold light of day brought an awful reality to the scene. Every window in our house was shattered and the frames loosened. Everything and everywhere was covered in a thick layer of dust contaminated with lumps of rubble and slivers of glass. What a nightmare for my house-proud mother!

To add to her anguish, I was in trouble, being unable to walk. Evidently, when those people in our cellar had been flung about, my right foot had slammed against the wall at the end of my bed. Relaxed by sleep the ankle had suffered impact damage to the cartilage between the bones.

This was obviously a job for the local hospital, but getting there presented a problem. With debris still straddling the road the bus service that normally passed our shop had been diverted. Dad reckoned he may be able to cadge a lift in one of the A.R.P vehicles, but they were all too busy. With no alternative I hopped along on one leg hanging on to dad until we reached the nearest bus diversion stage.

The scene at the hospital was pretty chaotic with staff overstretched by more urgent casualties. I recall that dad tried to distract me, but there was no disguising the fact that some trolleys being wheeled around contained very seriously injured people, with at least one covered completely with a blanket.

By comparison, I felt a bit of a fraud. We had to be patient. Eventually I was fixed up with heavy strapping that remained in place for many months. Opinion was, that the ankle should have been put in plaster, but none was available due to the heavy demand.

In later life I needed verification that I had attended the hospital that day but there was no record in the archives. Recalling the frantic situation that prevailed in that casualty department, I was not at all surprised!

This ankle was to remain a problem throughout my life, with an inherant weakness. Not a permanent handicap at that young age, as I guess that some cartilage regenerated, but it was always weak. Any uneven surface and over it went – Ouch!

When the time came for me to do National Service at the age of 18 I mentioned all this at the medical but it fell on deaf ears. They had heard every excuse in the book – and a few more!
'You can walk and breathe can't you? – Get out, you are A1!'

The only time that this caused me real grief was during 'Square-bashing', or initial training as it was politely termed. I stumbled and committed the cardinal sin of dropping my rifle. The drill instructor went completely berserk, but it was no good making excuses, just get on with it.
Four times around the parade ground in full pack, holding the rifle above my head made certain that never again would I drop the thing!

In later life however, Osteo-Arthritis set in and after limping for so long I was forced to retire a little early with a disability that now affects other joints and bits and pieces.

A mobility 'buggy' gets me out and about to terrorise the local community!

Having digressed, I must now revert back to the morning after the night before. A young soldier stood guard outside our shop with rifle and fixed bayonet to deter any would be looter. Anyone caught stealing from bomb damaged premises could be shot on sight! On reflection, this young lad was probably a member of the Home Guard.

My mothers pride and joy, the back garden greenhouse was not a pretty sight. All the vegetable plants being nurtured through the winter months were either mashed by glass or rubble, or had been blown away. No flowers to worry about, growing was for eating.

I was not much help but tried to join in the big clear up which mum had already started at first light. By now it was late morning and despite the chaotic jumble of stock, dust and rubble in the shop, dad decided to open for business. We were open already, like no door or windows!

Mum could not believe it and stomped around muttering "The man is mad". A few odd people turned up, more to see what had happened, but if they asked for any goods, dad scrabbled around on hands and knees in an effort to satisfy.

Really, my parents were the epitomé of the spirit that prevailed in those dark days. A determination to carry on regardless whatever the circumstances, compounded by a severe lack of sleep.

Gradually, concerted hard work throughout the day restored a semblance of order. Large metal bins had been placed on the pavement for rubbish and rubble. A constant stream of lorries shuttled back and forth removing the huge pile of masonry and debris that straddled the main road. Remarkably, this was re-opened for traffic by late afternoon.

This was obviously a very large calibre bomb, capable of widespread damage. Thankfully, some of the force had been dissipated by the width of the bridge, but the station was in a very sorry state.

A.R.P records in the borough archives confirm that this was a parachute mine, one of the largest and most powerful devices. This now explains the loud 'Crack' heard by my family upstairs in the kitchen. It was probably the parachute snapping open to support the 1 ton warhead swinging below.

Interestingly, the incident location is recorded as 'Between Sunderland Road – opposite our shop – and the station'. Had that Air Raid Warden scribe been correct it would have been straight down our chimney pot!

A copy of the appropriate Air Raid Wardens log book is shown overleaf.

UXB or UXS indicates an unexploded bomb or anti-aircraft shell. The significant entry is underlined.

Researching the borough archives I located a thick bundle of 'Incident Reports' and telephone message records relating to the scene.

Unfortunately, these are now rather fragile and cannot be re-produced. In fact, I had to don a pair of white linen gloves in order to view the pages.

It is of interest to quote from two of the more significant telephone message pages.

'27th September 1940. Time 02.03. Supplementary report.
Corner of Dorset Road and South Ealing Road.
Water Board required immediately. People trapped in cellars and in danger of drowning. Origin. Wardens Post B2'.

02.25. Supplementary report.
Extra heavy rescue squad required. Urgent.

LOG BOOK

DATE	INC.NO.	POSITION OF OCCURRENCE	TYPE of BOMB
26.9.40	30	6, Conway Crescent.	UXS.
"	32	7, Glenfield Terrace	UXB
"	33	West End Farn, Northolt	U.X.B & S.
"	34	Ealing Common Hard Courts, Western Gardens	H.E.
"	2	Popes Lane	2 land mine
27.9.40	3	South Ealing Road. N. of Station	H.E.
"	5	Sunderland Road, and South Ealing Stion	Land mine
"	5	19 & 21, Sunderland Road.	INC.
"	6	West Ealing Station	U.X.B.
"	7	64, Grove Avenue	H.E.
"	8	Greenford Avenue, adjoining Shakespeare Rd	U.X.B
"	9	54 & 56, Beresford Avenue	"
"	10	23, Grove Avenue	H.E.
"	11	Rear of Park Hotel, Greenford Avenue.	"
"	13	Scotch Common.	U.X.B.
"	14	Junction of Argyle Road & Crossways.	U.X.B & S.
"	15	203, Argyle Road	U.X.B
"	16	Highland Avenue, Hanwell	"
"	17	Boston Manor Road	"
"	1	8, Salvia Gardens	U.X.S.
28.9.40	2	Junction of Stanley Avenue, & Birkbeck Ave.	Shell
"	3	9, Spencer Close, West Twyford.	UXB or S.
"	1	Byron Hotel, Ruislip Road, Northolt	U.X.B.
"	2	Police Station & shop adjoining	INC.
"	3	Ealing Broadway.	"
"	4	Longfield Depot & Garage opposite.	"
"	5	Western Avenue junction with Hanger Hill	"
"	6	The Grove & E. of Grove Road.	"
"	7	No.1 Gordon Road	"
"	8	'Queen Victoria' & Police Station Billiard Hall Bond St. Mattock Lane Garage	"
"	9	Sayers Stores, Spring Bridge Road.	"
"	10	11 Webster Gardens	"

LOOK AND LISTEN. AS DAWN BREAKS THE SEARCH FOR SURVIVORS CONTINUES.

LATER THAT DAY. THE ROAD IS NOW CLEARED FOR VEHICLE ACCESS AS THE RESCUE SQUADS, NOW IN THE BACKGROUND, TAKE A WELL EARNED REST BREAK OUTSIDE OUR SHOP WHERE MY MOTHER SERVED REFRESHMENTS. THE MAN IN THE FOREGROUND WEARING A CLOTH CAP, IS ALMOST CERTAINLY MY FATHER. THE SCHOOL AUXILIARY FIRE STATION WAS BEHIND THE BRICK WALL ON THE RIGHT.

A PRESENT DAY PHOTOGRAPH TAKEN FROM ALMOST EXACTLY THE SAME LOCATION.

It remained an unexplained phenomenon how all our shelter occupants had been picked up and hurled forward. Without logical explanation it could only be some effect of being underground. Sometimes, blast had the most extraordinary effects. There are many tales of people being stripped naked of clothes yet remaining unhurt.

Meals were now a problem. Minute particles of glass had infiltrated every possible nook and cranny. Mum was so apprehensive that despite a most stringent examination of food, a piece may be missed. Due to the severe rationing provisions could not be thrown away. We ate so very carefully for many days, to constant entreaties from mum, 'Eat slowly, chew it up well'.

The shop windows were covered with corrugated iron sheets. Some of our more obscure windows were boarded up permanently. Only where necessary was glass replaced.

The storage area for the Paraffin oil tanks was also covered with corrugated iron sheeting, which would at least provide a more substantial protection from an incendiary bomb.

Dad had a sale of 'Blitz' damaged goods, which included the flying oil stove. This went well and suggestions were made to the bank and off-licence that they should follow suit!

That reminds me that all the smashed stock from the off-licence left the area smelling like a gigantic cocktail. The fumes were such that I guess we all walked around with a silly but happy grin on our faces.

Things were slowly getting back to normality, whatever that may be now, or for the uncertain future.

It was only quite recently that I met a lady who, as an 18 year old, lived about a quarter of a mile away near St Mary's Church. They had of course, heard and felt the massive explosion, but had no idea where this had occurred.

As she left home to go to work next morning she was horrified to see clothing festooned on the surrounding trees and lying in the street. In the half light of early morning, one can now well understand her initial shock and conclusion.

Evidently she spent the day at work fretting about the gruesome possibilities, eventually relieved to find out that one of the shops destroyed was a gents outfitters. Somehow, the blast effect had deposited much of the stock to that particular area.

By now, both my brothers were settled into forces life. Bern had been called up first as the youngest, but Ted soon followed and was now an airframe fitter. Later in the war his carpentry talents were ideally employed repairing the all wooden Mosquito aircraft.

Bern, the 'Happy go lucky' character of the family, became a driver mechanic in the Royal Army Service Corps.

My parents were incredulous when he eventually rose to the rank of Regimental Sergeant Major.

The look on mum's face was a picture when he walked into the shop one morning, then resplendent in Corporal stripes – followed by 19 more drivers! "Hi Mum" he exclaimed, "I told the lads where we could get a decent cuppa and a civilised wee".

As the lead driver of a convoy heading South, he brought them through Ealing and parked the lot down an adjacent side road.

Despite the restrictions of tea rationing, mum made them all a welcome brew. After they had left she was pleasantly surprised to find four new packets beside the caddy.

Food rationing was now quite severe. Meat was included from March 1940, starting at one shilling, two penny worth. About 7 pence in today's terms. This was to shrink even further as conditions worsened.

The original butter portion of 2 ounces was halved and the cheese allowance was more suited to a mouse-trap. Eggs went from 2 per week, to 1 every second week.

For most people, 2 ounces of tea per week was the hardest imposition to bear, for a good old cuppa solved everything.

For us kids, only 3 ounces of sweets was a disaster. We tended to choose the hardest, like 'Gobstoppers' to make them last longer. You got about 9 'normal' sized sweets such as boiled fruits for your allowance. One sweet and a few sucks of another each day!

Some things remained off ration. My mother constantly queued with great patience for rabbit or fish when available. There was a very effective 'Housewives Grapevine' that rapidly spread the news of a delivery to the fishmonger, whatever it might be.

If a queue was seen to be forming, whatever the shop, housewives would join in with hope that some unexpected 'goodies' would be available.

Soup was always a mainstay. It seemed to me that throughout the entire war years a saucepan was permanently simmering on the kitchen range. Mum would re-cycle any bones or scraps left over such as bacon rinds to produce tasty and nutritious broth, topped with small lumps of crust from the National Wholemeal bread loaf. Mother's visionary croutons!

Milk was now becoming scarce and strictly rationed. The adult allowance became 2½ pints per week, so anyone on their own would have half a pint for five days, then go without.
It was priced at 4½ pence for a pint – about 2p in today's money.

As with many deliveries such as coal and bread, milk was delivered door to door by a horse drawn vehicle.
My aunt drove a milk float throughout the war years.

Ration books were printed on very inferior rag-like paper. The coupons were cut out by the shopkeeper.
Later on points coupons were introduced for so-called luxury items such as tinned food, jam, rice, biscuits etc, to a total of 20 points per person per month. This gave the housewife a limited choice to

supplement the staple allowances. This was not wildly exciting as for example, a tin of corned beef gobbled up 12 points.

Bacon and ham were additional to the meat ration, but only 4 ounces of either could be purchased.

At the end of the day, the ration for one person per week would hardly fill a plate in our affluent times.

Soap was also rationed. 3 ounces of toilet, or 6 ounces of powder. Any scraps left over were warmed in a pan, then mashed together. It became my job to press the slimy mess into match boxes to set.

It was only in later years that I began to understand and appreciate that my mother obviously went without to ensure that I had sufficient to eat. Food may have lacked variety but I am now sure that nutritional items found their way to my plate. This would also explain why mum often said "It's okay, I'm not hungry".

I reckon that the vast majority of mothers would have adopted the same unselfish philosophy.

Frugality became second nature. My sister melted lipstick ends to fashion another stick. Women were officially encouraged to 'Look their best'. I am not sure about this, but I do remember her messing about with some beetroot juice which may have been an alternative to rouge or 'blusher'.

Paper was precious. Letters were written both sides, edge to edge. Brown paper was smoothed out to live another day. Even string was never cut, but carefully un-knotted to use again.

Newspapers shrunk from 8 to 6 pages. Once read they were cut up into squares , looped with string and hung up in the toilet. No-one could think of any further use after that....yet!

Fruit virtually disappeared, unless it was home grown. Oranges and bananas vanished for years. When they did re-appear after the war many children had never seen one and tried to eat them with the skins on.

Fish was not rationed except by great scarcity. As with every aspect of life, food was controlled by a government ministry who advertised in every way possible the latest 'Food Flash'.

The theme was always, 'It will do you good'.

At one time the populace were encouraged to eat carrots to improve night vision in the black-out. They told us that fighter pilots were munching them like rabbits, but the truth of the matter was that the country was running short of potatoes!

The sale of white bread was then prohibited with the official explanation that it was unhealthy and lacked vitamins. The replacement was called 'National Wholemeal'. A brown, gritty, lumpy product that thoroughly deserved the uncomplimentary names bestowed upon it which are better left to the imagination!

To ensure that everyone was adequately nourished, what were called 'British Restaurants' were set up, where workers could get a basic meal at reasonable cost. A typical dish would be minced beef - goes further! - with potato. To add some flavour there would be a variation of turnips, swedes, parsnips, whatever was available.

At school we were fortunate for a while until supplies ran out, to receive a daily dose of cod liver oil – Ugh! – or orange juice.

We also had a half pint of milk every morning for a short period.

By now it had become compulsory for everyone, including children, to carry an identity card. The number became indelibly printed in the mind and even now, after more than 60 years, I have no hesitation in recalling DWPB 174/3.

Nothing sums up the spirit of those dark days quite like the characters, catch phrases and songs that came over the wireless. Tommy Handley led the hugely popular I.T.M.A – 'It's that man again' with the unforgetable voices of Mrs Mopp and Colonel Chinstrap.

The catch phrases from this show became part of everyday language. 'Can I do you now sir' – 'Ta Ta for now' 'I don't mind if I do'.

I remember reading somewhere that a little lad buried beneath the rubble of his house greeted his rescuers with the words "Can you do me now sir".

News readers such as Alvar Liddel, Frank Phillips and John Snagg became house-hold names as they identified themselves on every occasion to deter Nazi pirate broadcasts from impersonating them.

Towards the end of the 'Blitz' I may have been registered once again as a 'slightly injured' statistic.

During a daylight raid I nipped into the back garden to see what was going on. Just as I walked past mum's shattered greenhouse a nearby 'bang' dislodged a broken pane of glass which dropped, pointed end downwards, straight into the soft part of my leg above the knee.

The main part broke off as it did so and as I pulled out the remainder blood spurted everywhere. Boy, was I scared!

What a panic. It is not difficult to understand the reaction of my mother as this was the same leg that had suffered ankle injury a few weeks earlier.

Having stemmed the flow by a tight bandage above the wound it was another bus ride to the hospital. 'Oh no, - not you again!' The hole was stitched together. It was very painful but I was quite proud of my war wound.

Even now, the round white knobular scar is still visible.

At least it gave dad the required impetus to knock out all the remaining broken glass from the greenhouse – or was that mum?.

A MASSIVE BOMB CRATER AT EALING ELECTRICITY WORKS POPES LANE. OCTOBER 1940

Everyone was mad about the wartime songs. Had there been 'Pop Charts' then Bing Crosby would have been up there with Anne Shelton. A host of songs became hits to cheer up battle weary Britain. They included 'Coming In On A Wing And A Prayer' – 'Wish Me Luck As You Wave Me Goodbye' – 'Praise The Lord And Pass The Ammunition' and of course 'Kiss Me Goodnight Sergeant Major' and 'Roll Out The Barrel'.

Love songs and those looking forward to peace were the most popular. Classics such as 'We'll Meet Again' – 'I'll Be Seeing You' and the 'White Cliffs Of Dover' were the hallmark of Vera Lynne, the 'Sweetheart of the forces'.

One comedian that I was not allowed to listen to was Max Miller. His jokes were considered so blue, but I guess would now be acceptable at a vicarage tea party. Mum thought that he was a dreadful person. Dad mumbled something about "He's alright, I reckon a good turn".

Nowadays, a radio is either a blaring cacophony of noise wielded by some inconsiderate youth, or idly listened to as a background. It is therefore difficult to comprehend the total attention that we paid, grouped around the wireless set.

People declared that the Germans timed their attacks to coincide with the best programmes, for the transmitters shut down at the onset of a raid. In the middle of I.T.M.A that was really pushing their luck!

As Autumn turned to winter the Blitz raged on, night after night until everything seemed to merge together. Early one evening I argued with my Aunt Emily who was visiting. She said "The sirens have gone" I said "Yeh, it's the All-Clear". "No, the warning". I was certain I was right until aircraft were heard and the guns opened up.

"Er, OK, sorry Auntie, you could be right". On that particular evening the sirens sounded the alert and All-clear in confused sequence as nine separate raids were launched with short intervals between. This seemed to be a deliberate ploy to fray still further the jangled nerves of embattled Londoners.

It is incredible how one can recall the most insignificant moments of life, but that argument with my Aunt preceded what I feel must have been my first really original joke.

Although the kitchen windows were still boarded up, mum had sorted out some replacement curtains, as she said "To cheer the place up a bit". These were covered with a bold floral pattern.

My Aunt said "I like your mum's new curtains, are they Hydrangeas?" I replied, "No, Hide der winders".

Christmas was approaching, but this was hardly a season of goodwill to all men. We could think of a few exceptions!

This was to be a very austere occasion. To our surprise, mother announced "I am going to make a cake". We all looked at each other, "A what- what with?" dad exclaimed!

Not being involved I have no idea of the ultimate ingredients, but do know that carrots, powdered egg and National Wholemeal breadcrumbs featured strongly. It certainly looked good. Taste?, well debatable is the word, but we scoffed the lot.

The cellar was decorated with simple paper chains that various people found left over from previous years. At least they provided something different for occupational therapy in the evenings as the 'young-uns' stuck each one together.

Christmas cards were not sent through the post and not being made anyway. This would constitute a waste of valuable time and paper. However, the Newsagents along the road found a couple of pre-war packs and for a laugh we gave one to each of our regular shelter guests, captioned 'Thank you for sleeping with us'.

I do recall that with the other 2 youngsters in the cellar, we made some 'Bon-Bons' as they were called (Crackers) with odd bits of coloured paper around a cardboard tube. Handwritten silly jokes were inserted, together with any odd small items we could find.

No 'Crack' strips. Anything that went bang was put to a more practical use!

When pulled, we just shouted 'BANG'. We were easily pleased in those days!

With an acute shortage of so called 'Luxury' goods, presents were virtually out of the question. I do recall receiving several books, maybe second hand, and a beautiful wooden Spitfire carved by brother Ted. I now wonder – What happened to that?

I believe that this was the first occasion that I was allowed an alcoholic drink. The off-licence gave a bottle of Sherry to each of the three cellar shelters and this was shared out as a special treat.

The original great fire of London began in a bakery in Pudding Lane in the year 1666. On the night of December 29th 1940, the second started from the sky.

The evening remained ominously quiet. No sirens sounded as the hours ticked by. People questioned the unusual lull. 'Where are the buggers – what are they up to tonight?'

It was almost a relief when the alert sounded at about 11.30 pm. This was normality, now we can settle down.

That however, was not to be, for what ensued proved to be a new dimension of horror.

History records that only 150 enemy aircraft were employed in a brief half-hour raid, but each was loaded to capacity with small incendiary bombs that cascaded down in their thousands to create a sea of fire in the central and Eastern areas of the capital.

Down the shelter we could hear the droning 'planes and the constant thud of anti-aircraft fire, but something was different. Why no 'crump' of high explosives?

Again came the mystified questions. 'What the hell's going on up there?'. Finally, curiosity got the better of dad and others who ventured up to the street entrance and peered out, to be confronted by a night sky transformed into a bubbling cauldron of fire as the incendiaries whispered down to ignite in myriad flares of white hot magnesium. I heard their gasps of 'Oh my God, look at that!'

Whether by accident or design, the Germans had timed the attack well. We now know that the Thames was at its lowest ebb and with many water mains already ruptured by earlier bombs, thousands of coupled up hoses snaked through the streets into the river around the docks and city area.

To add to the difficulties, an unexploded parachute mine was nestling in the mud near St Paul's Cathedral.

Many incendiaries fell on the Cathedral, but were dealt with by the firewatchers and other volunteers who came to help. Their valiant efforts saved the Wren masterpiece from destruction to stand as a symbol of faith throughout the war.

Before long, the multitude of hoses drained the remaining water from the Thames and as they began to suck up sloshy mud the firefighters could only stand and watch as the city burned.

The helpless firemen could only resume the battle from about 4.00am when the tide began to flow back, but by then, huge swathes of buildings were beyond salvation as the unchecked flames roared out across alleys and streets seeking out new buildings to add to the inferno.

Came the dawn and thousands of bleary eyed Londoners emerged from the Underground stations and other places of refuge to make their way to work, to be confronted by a nightmare scene obscured by a thick choking fog of acrid smoke and ash. Coughing and spluttering, they picked their way through debris and a tangle of hoses through a maze of obstructed streets with buildings still ablaze, only to find that offices and other places of employment had gone forever.

Despite the carnage that already existed, we now know that fortune actually smiled on London. A second wave of bombers following up the initial attack was recalled due to a thick bank of fog that rolled in over the English Channel. One can only now wonder at this divine intervention.

In our area there was little sleep for the grown-ups that night as groups went outside to locate and deal with the devices that had fallen locally from wayward aircraft that had missed the main target area of the city. Many had fallen in roads and were left to burn themselves out. We were so very fortunate, the only real incident was a burning garden shed which they extinguished.

The All-Clear sounded quite quickly around midnight. All the people in our cellar trooped up to the top of our house to gaze out over London in dumbstruck awe. That scene will stay in my mind's eye for evermore. The entire skyline had been transformed into a pulsating sea of fire, interposed with flares of brilliant red embers as buildings or roofs collapsed.

It was later revealed that the huge red glow in the sky could be seen from over 60 miles away along the coast.

Some fires were burning in our vicinity and the air was stifling with acrid ash as a gentle breeze wafted the polluted hot air ever closer. 'Those poor devils' was an oft quoted phrase as we returned to our shelter haven with heavy hearts.

Sleep was impossible. Even down the cellar we could now smell the smoke fumes, constantly reviving a mental picture of the fiery hell that we had witnessed.

Of course, the persistent tang of smoke worried everyone. My parents were very agitated. Had an incendiary been missed somewhere. They could lodge in the most inaccessible places such as loft space.

Consequently, my parents, aided by friends from the shelter, dashed up and down stairs virtually all that long night, checking and re-checking.

Dawn came as a blessed relief and we were all up and about early. A massive pall of black smoke hung over the city like an umbrella. Here and there, flames could still be seen flickering skyward.

What a night! In the Western suburbs we could only fearfully imagine what it must be like in the heart of such devastation. We were now very apprehensive and afraid of what tonight may bring.

Arthur was on duty that night and our thoughts and prayers were with him. He did not arrive home at the usual time and we were filled with foreboding.

What a huge relief when he finally trudged through the door. Absolutely shattered, filthy dirty and soaking wet. He was too tired and choked with emotion to answer our eager questions. All he kept repeating was "It was hell on earth. Nothing we could do. Nothing, nothing. It was hopeless" Tears trickled down his cheeks.

Thankfully, the Luftwaffe never again repeated a firestorm raid of such intensity, but reverted to their normal tactics.

To while away the endless hours it was essential to do something by way of occupational therapy. Knitting was of course, a favourite among the ladies. I can still raise a few eyebrows by mentioning that I used to do knitting. As a lad, I even managed to produce sufficient coloured squares of old wool to complete a bedspread for my trestle bed. Another amusement was to thread wool around four nails in the top of a cotton reel. Somehow, a snake like coil emerged from the other end. This was then coiled and stitched to make table mats and the like.

This was shown to me by a young teenage girl named Jean. She had been in a dance hall above a large departmental store in Ealing when this was blasted by one of the larger devices to fall on the Borough, another parachute mine.

Two entire streets were devastated and the area did not recover for many years after the war. After lying waste for a long time, it is now the site of a multi-storey car park among blocks of flats.

The large plate glass windows burst inward causing many horrendous injuries. I was fascinated by this young lady's injuries, yet horrified until I became used to them. Her arms and hands were a mass of chunky knobular scars graduating from white to a deep purple, like the hide of some prehistoric animal. These were sustained when she instinctively flung up her arms to protect her face. It was almost a miracle that only two slivers penetrated her forehead. It was rumoured that several people were decapitated.

The wisdom of holding a dance in such dangerous times may well be questioned, but people were prepared to take calculated risks in order to find some enjoyment. On this occasion the dancing couples relaxed as an enemy aircraft passed overhead and the engine noise faded away.

The band struck up again with what proved to be a symphony of death as the huge canister silently floated down under its silken canopy.

The local Wardens post, designated B2, was situated in a corner of the senior school playground and constantly manned on a duty rota basis. What with the shop, school caretaking, firewatching etc, how on earth did my father find the time to be an Air Raid Warden? Generally, people had by now adapted to less sleep, as apart from the noise of the raids, so many duties had to be undertaken by night. The word 'Stress' was not familiar to the English language in those days and would probably have been laughed off anyway!

I got to know all the Wardens quite well and was allowed into the post, providing that I kept out of the way. Actually, this was not so easy, as the blockhouse type structure was very confined. Maybe only about ten feet square, reduced by the desk and chairs. I would go in there after school and try to make myself useful by running errands. At least mum knew where to find me.

The activity was interesting and one got prior warning of a raid. The telephone would ring with the brief message 'Air Raid Warning Yellow'. This meant that raiders had crossed the coast, also the cue for me to be slung out! If the target proved to be London, the timing was such that I would arrive home just as the sirens sounded.

I was still too young, but lads of fourteen were engaged as messenger boys, provided they had a bicycle. This was quite a hazardous task as they were required to carry out their duties throughout a raid, particularly if telephone communications had been disrupted.

Wardens post B2 still exists to this day, probably now relegated to some mundane storage purpose.

Despite the constant threat of attack, it is remarkable how life continued a pattern of normality that even extended to us kids going out to play around the streets, but never without the stern finger wagging warning "Not too far away and straight back if the sirens sound". "Yeh, Yeh, OK mum".

The period between leaving school at about 4.pm and six was usually quiet, but it was of course dark during the winter months. It was not until the evenings lengthened at the approach of Spring 1941 that we could get out in daylight for a while unless it was a holiday period.

One incident still concerns me as a totally illogical and out of character escapade that could have caused my parents much grief. A group of us kids were chasing around the local alleys looking for something to do. Collecting shrapnel or whatever, was now 'old hat'. We all had plenty and any interesting bits would have been found on our way to school in the morning.

Our wanderings took us to the vicinity of the access road where the first bomb had fallen in our area. The surrounding houses looked very forlorn, with shattered windows and roofs. Most were structurally sound and remain to this day with the exception of five which were eventually demolished and rebuilt to a new design. At that time, all the families had been moved out into temporary accommodation until the overworked repair gangs could get round to this area.

The odd remaining pane of glass presented an appealing target and I guess it was inevitable that one of the lads – not me – would try his aim with a stone. Crash! What a shot. We were impressed. In those days we were not destructive by nature or inclination. We had already seen enough to last a lifetime.

For some reason however, the situation got a bit out of hand as we all began to throw stones.

Suddenly the cry rang out "Look out, it's the rozzers".

We all scattered round the maze of alleys. I was still limping but reasonably mobile. There were few young coppers about, many were in the armed forces and those chasing us didn't stand a chance. I was scared stiff that I may have been recognised and when a policeman came into the shop later that day I rocketed out the back way at high speed! How was I to know that he was just a normal customer?

It is indicative of our total respect for law and order in those days, that it remains such a vivid recollection of miscreant youth. My one consolation is, that I did not actually do any damage. Certainly I threw stones, but only to avoid being called a 'Cissie'. They all reckoned I was just a rotten shot.

Floating paper boats in the portable fire fighting reservoirs was a far more normal pastime to vary the now selective search for souvenirs. We had become far more discerning collectors and on one occasion I gained the envy of all my mates.

Just round the corner from home, there lying in the gutter was the entire nose cone of an anti-aircraft shell, complete with timing ring. It was virtually undamaged and how this survived intact from its explosive journey skyward and back defies all logic.

It must have been about this time that the Germans started dropping thousands of metallic strips. Black on one side, silver the other, these nine inch strips evidently distorted the Radar and other locating devices. Initially we rushed around collecting the stuff but soon realised that we could finish up knee deep as it littered the streets. Mum was pleased, having already commented that we had no intention of re-papering any room!

For some reason, maybe a holiday or week-end, I was out and about on my bike at mid-morning. The sirens sounded but by now daylight raids were rarely serious, so I bade a casual farewell to my mates 'See you later' and turned for home.

Suddenly I became aware of an ever increasing deep throated roar of aero engines from somewhere behind. As I turned in some alarm, a dark sinister Heinkel bomber swept low over the rooftops firing staccato bursts of machine gun fire. As I flung myself off the bike I glimpsed the evil looking black crosses on the wings.

Diving into the scant protection of a garden wall, a line of bullets stitched a way up the road. In those split seconds as shattered tarmac, stones and bullets whined in all directions, I was petrified and ashamed to be sobbing with fright. Fearful that anyone should see me in that state, I hid in an alley until sufficiently composed to go home. As I did so, two 'Spits' roared over in hot pursuit. "Get him, the rotten basket" I yelled – well, something like that. Good job mum wasn't around to hear it!

Doubtful that I was the prime target, a line of stationary army lorries in the adjoining main road provided the likely objective of that wayward shooting.

The morning after a raid was always the time to exchange information on local 'Hits'. "Have you heard? – big one in blank street or UXB in so and so road, some dead they reckon". Did we know anyone there? One morning at school, the little blonde girl that I fancied did not arrive. Sadly, she never would again.

The entire family had been killed by a direct hit on the house and Anderson garden shelter.

I was so sad. This was the first time that I had been affected personally. The harsh realities of war were fast catching up with this young lad.

Sometimes I helped the lady from the 'cycle shop alongside the underground station to tend her allotment. As mentioned earlier, every spare inch of soil was cultivated to produce vegetables. With German 'U' Boats sinking many cargo vessels bringing food to Britain,the slogan 'Grow Your Own' was becoming a vital necessity. Lily's plot was hazardous to say the least. It was situated inside the boundary fence of the railway on top of the embankment. Protected by only a few strands of wire stretched between two posts, one false step would result in a tumble down the steep slope to the electrified lines below. Any lifted spuds could become instant fries!

To reach the allotment it was necessary to climb over her garden fence. It was then a ritual that I was asked to turn my back in case I should catch a glimpse of her undies as she cocked her leg over the fence.

How on earth did my mother allow me to be exposed to either hazard!

In the years to come it was Lily's father who made a personal introduction that secured my first job at the age of fourteen, to work in the stores of the A.E.C factory in Southall.

In peacetime they were the builders of London buses, but at the time of my employment to revitalise their war effort, production was geared to Matador field gun tractors and specialist fighting vehicles, but that is a later story.

Meanwhile, our cellar shelter was becoming a little more home from home. The various regular families vied with each other to provide a cosy corner. The walls and beams were distempered pale blue. No such thing as emulsion paint in those days.

The ladies reckoned that this colour made the place seem even colder. A few pictures were hung, but without glass to avoid the shatter hazard. Most were photographs of loved ones away in the forces.

Odd items of personal furniture were permitted, but confined to a chair or any small item that did not encroach beyond the allotted space for each bunk.

As previously mentioned, I attended the lectures at the school and became particularly adept at aircraft recognition and fire fighting.

There was no doubt that if, or more likely when, the occasion arose, I would take my place as the 'hoseman', wriggling along on knees and elbows with a dustbin lid in one hand to shield the head and the stirrup pump hose in the other, searching for the base of the incendiary blaze. The main problem at an early stage would be the intense white glare produced by the burning magnesium. This would torture the eyes.

The metal dustbin lid was vital, not only as a protection against the glare. but to resist a tendency for small explosive charges to be incorporated into the bomb to disperse globules of fiery venom.

It was my job to keep the fire fighting equipment around the house in good order. Buckets always topped up with sand or water. The stirrup pump greased. A garden hose was kept neatly coiled beneath the kitchen sink. Any wasted seconds could prove vital.

Another reason for enjoying the lectures, now being held in late afternoon, was that the instructor had a film projector and a collection of silent films.

One remains a vivid memory to this day, titled 'Q Ships'. This was the story of converted and disguised merchant ships in the first great war of 1914-18. By their innocent appearance they lured German 'U' Boats to the surface to finish them off with gunfire rather than waste torpedoes.

As the submarine closed range, sudden activity aboard the merchantman saw tarpaulin covers ripped off deck mounted guns which immediately opened fire on the sub'. What a cheer went up as the first shot blew off the conning tower.

It had been a lovely clear but bitterly cold evening as we made our way to a lecture. My hands were freezing, but in those days boys did not wear gloves. It was 'Cissie'.

Such rare clear night skies were always a cause for worry. It was perfect conditions for night bombing and we knew that a raid was inevitable.

One feature had become apparent, that with the total blackout and literally no light reflection, the night sky took on a velvety hue with hundreds of hitherto unseen stars twinkling like tiny diamonds. It was not unusual to see shooting stars which under normal circumstances would probably have been missed.

It could well have been that very evening when the sirens sounded just as we were ready to return home, about ten minutes walk away. We had only just set out when the familiar distinctive drone of enemy aircraft became louder.

Suddenly, a parachute flare burst into glaring brilliance directly overhead, turning night into day.

The three of us stood transfixed as though exposed naked in the street.

Instinctively one felt that this was something personal and if we dared to move, retribution would surely follow.

Common sense prevailed as we joined hands to run the gauntlet to our shelter haven, but all the while sneaking an odd glance upward.

Searchlights were adding to the brilliance of the scene and in an instant one latched onto the aircraft like a tiny moth shimmering amid the stars. Immediately, multiple beams converged on this rare visual target to form an inescapable pool of white light.

Simultaneously, every 'Ack-Ack' gun within range opened up a curtain of fire.

Almost home by now, we paused to gaze fascinated by the tortuous seemingly slow motion turning and twisting of the 'plane as it tried in vain to escape the clutching fingers of light.

It seemed inevitable that one of the twinkling shell bursts would find the target. Gradually we could discern a red glow as the now stricken aircraft rolled away and began to descend with a comet like tail of flame.

The searchlights moved away. The guns fell silent. It was almost an act of reverence as a multitude of eyes must have watched and wondered about the fate of the crew in that now blazing inferno.

Roy Bartlett

If we could rely on the rumours next morning, it finally came to earth in open fields many miles away.

As mentioned earlier, my cat Stripey was a crafty old thing with a total aversion to the sirens.

With typical feline cunning and independence he figured out his own private air-raid shelter. In the upstairs bath!

We tried coaxing or carrying him down to the cellar shelter, but he would have none of that and cried at the top of the stairs until someone relented and let him out to race upstairs to the bathroom.

This was not a problem. We were quite happy to go along with his enterprising arrangement. That is, until the day that mother was running a bath.

Baths had to be taken whenever an opportunity presented itself, with no guarantee that just as you got in the sirens would not sound.

Fortunately the water was not very deep as officially we were only allowed four inches in order to conserve fuel and water.

In the meantime the sirens did sound. As usual, Stripey rocketed in through the back door, up the stairs and leapt over the side of the bath straight into the hot water. What a commotion! Spitting and snarling at anyone within range, a sopping wet bedraggled excuse for a cat skidded through the house at 97 miles per hour. Finding the back door closed he accomplished a racing turn around my bemused mother and escaped out of the open shop doorway, not to be seen again for two days.

Never again did he venture to the bathroom and we reached an amicable solution by moving his box back to the original place beneath the scullery sink.

Despite all the difficulties, there were some lighter moments. In the shop was a large galvanised tin bath filled with bark chippings. The name sticks in my mind – 'Quassia Chips'.

I had no idea what these were for, until current curiosity prompted me to refer to a reference book. I started reading and became completely nonplussed by the definition. 'South American tree. The bark yields a bitter concoction used as a tonic'.

What was my father up to?

But, reading on it became clear. When soaked for a period, the residual liquid may be used as a pesticide.

So that was it, no such things as Greenfly spray cans in those days!

Anyway, I digress. One of our regular customers was a very portly gentleman who weighed around eighteen stone. Mum was alone in the shop at the time, when having made his purchase, he turned, stumbled and sat back heavily in the bath of chips where he became immovably wedged.

Trying desperately not to laugh, but with tears running down her face, mum tugged and pulled to no avail. Calling me to assist only made matters worse. I had no inhibitions and collapsed in a fit of the giggles. The poor chap was grunting and groaning in desperate attempts to get out. Eventually, mum enlisted the help of passers-by and a combined heave-ho was successful.

One thing is for sure. No greenfly on his rear end for a while!.

Into 1941 and clothes rationing was introduced. The adult allowance of 66 coupons had to be spread over a year and every need.

For example, a man's overcoat took 16 coupons.

The requirement to economise on material resulted in a straight knee length skirt for the ladies. Men were limited to three pockets on a jacket, with no buttons on the cuffs, or turn-ups on the 19 inch trouser bottoms.

Clothes were improvised from all sorts of unusual materials, from parachute silk to dyed blankets for overcoats.

Despite these restrictions, clothing was in short supply anyway. All the manufacturers were geared fully to the production of uniforms and combat dress for the forces. Make do and mend was the order of the day. My mother certainly had adequate occupational therapy to while away the shelter time, stitching, sewing and darning a never ending pile of garments. – Usually mine!

My sister was always good for a laugh as she carefully tanned her legs with the dregs of the teapot which she meticulously saved. With the gradual disappearance of stockings, the girls improvised with gravy browning or tea. Ivy favoured tea as this was more permanent. Gravy browning tended to have interesting variations when it rained or attracted sniffing dogs!

The illusion was completed by carefully tracing a seam up the back of the leg with a black pencil. There was never a shortage of volunteers for this job, but usually left to a good friend.

I must have been a real problem, constantly scuffing out the soles of my shoes playing football in the playground.

It was almost impossible to buy a new pair, consequently dad had to use his fast diminishing stock of stick-on rubber soles to do yet another cover-up job.

Sister Ivy arrived home brandishing a pair of the new fangled 'Utility' shoes. These had a lightweight wooden sole with canvas upper straps. She immediately found these to be slippery on wet surfaces and noisy, definitely not designed for creeping about. The constant clackety-clack around the house drove us all mad. In sheer desperation dad cut some strips of rubber from an old cycle inner tube and stuck them on as 'silencers'.

It must have been in late 1940 that my brother Bern accomplished a motor cycle journey home that could be more graphically likened to the old fairground 'Wall of Death' ride.

With a valued 48 hour pass in his pocket he set out from his Essex camp on a bitterly cold night with snow in the air. As he made his way through London a raid was in progress and bombs were falling all around. In the inky blackness of the black-out, progress was slow. Just as well! Peering ahead with just a filtered glow from the headlight he did not see the gaping bomb crater ahead and in total shock and fright drove straight down the steep side. Having regained some composure he struggled to lug the heavy bike out and resumed his journey, none the worse apart from grazes and bruises.

By the time that he arrived home he was in a very sorry state, virtually frozen to the machine. Bern shuffled in, bent over and with his hands in a rigid grip position. His face was contorted with frozen pain and I recall the glaze of ice that had formed on his clothing and the sparkling rime on his face around his goggles that gave the appearance of an Arctic explorer.

Once thawed out he had to endure a tongue lashing lecture from mum for being so foolhardy. As he was by now engaged to Joyce it can only be hoped that his crazy escapade was worthwhile!

It was raining when I came home from school one lunch-time and I could see that water was pouring over the top gutter. Mentioning this to dad, he said "I know, I've asked old George to have a look at it". George was the local 'Handy Andy'.

He duly arrived the following day and clambered up the ladder with a scoop and bucket. As usual, I was being nosy and watching from below. Suddenly 'Old George' descended the ladder with remarkable speed. As he reached the bottom rungs I could see that something was wrong. His face was white and one hand was clamped to his mouth. Racing to the kerb he was violently sick in the gutter.

I thought that he had supped a few too many down the pub, but I was hastily ushered out of the way, despite protests and mounting curiosity. 'Earwigging' on whispered conversations I gradually figured out the grim grisly story, but it was not until many years later that my sister confirmed the details.

The poor man had found the gutter blocked at the down pipe joint with a jelly like substance. Trying to scoop this out it was not only clinging together, but attached was a mane of obviously human hair.

One could never be certain of course, but the awful reality had to relate to the family that were never found after the mine fell on the adjacent shops.

It was not until fairly recently that my sister-in-law Joyce told me that a woman's hand was found by workmen assisting my father to clear up outside the shop. Is it any wonder that my parents were anxious to keep things like that from me?

The war was not going well. Everyone expected the invasion to take place anytime. Every day that passed became a bonus. Speculation was the main theme of conversation. There was little more that could be done to add to a fierce determination to defend every inch of the land.

Winston Churchill's words of a few weeks earlier remained uppermost in everyone's mind. 'We shall never surrender'.

It was not until long after the war when records became available, that it was established that destiny had in fact been resolved way back on September 15th. On that day, now commemorated as 'Battle of Britain' day, the Germans hurled every available aircraft into the fray in a final effort to destroy the R.A.F.

They failed, the Luftwaffe suffered heavy losses and Hitler was finally forced to abandon his invasion plans codenamed 'Sealion'.

Earlier failure to gain mastery of the air, an essential ingredient for success, caused several postponements of the assault by sea and air, originally scheduled for early September.

The valiant R.A.F pilots continued to hold out against overwhelming odds and the date was revised to September 11th.

It was again re-scheduled to the 17th, but the disastrous losses sustained on the 15th finally convinced the German High Command to abandon the invasion.

One can only repeat that oft quoted Churchillian phrase – 'Never in the field of human conflict, has so much been owed by so many to so few'.

It was felt in some quarters that Hitler lacked a firm conviction to invade Britain. He knew the people! However, the British populace could see no other logical course of events and every day mused 'Why doesn't he come?'

History records that almost immediately, on September 19th, the massed barges, ships and troops began to disperse from the channel ports of France. Obviously, on the home front the population remained unaware of this turn of events and remained totally on edge every day.

During the daily air battles that changed the course of history and indeed, the way of life and liberty of the British people, the Luftwaffe lost 1389 aircraft of all types and suffered the loss of 2500 aircrew.

The R.A.F also paid dearly by the loss of 790 fighter planes with 554 pilots killed.

This present day photograph shows the Wardens post B2 still situated in the corner of what was then the senior school playground. Now a grubby and forlorn legacy of history. The original entrance on the right can be identified by a different shade of brickwork.

THE A.R.P WARDENS POST B2

Ealing was now being struck quite frequently. Within the now extended area of the Borough that encompasses Acton and Southall, a total of 1200 high explosive bombs fell throughout the duration of the war.

A further 46 were designated UXBs. Many of these were defused and rendered safe by the bomb disposal squad, but a few were fitted with the deadly delayed action fuse and subsequently exploded.

These figures include six 1 ton warhead parachute mines which caused so much widespread damage and casualties. Three more failed to explode.

It is impossible to even estimate the number of small incendiary bombs. These can only be numbered in thousands. However, statistics are recorded for the larger type of incendiary device known as an oil bomb of which 53 are detailed.

Of the civilian population within the current day borough boundary 490 people lost their lives with a further 19 unidentified.
Another 750 were seriously injured.

As school children we were warned about the possibility of a particularly nasty device called a 'Butterfly Bomb'.
This was a small canister about the size of a large food can, with a pair of outstretched wing panels.
They were specifically designed to harm the person. In modern terminology I guess they would be called anti-personnel mines. The shape was unfamiliar and intriguing to inquisitive kids. Some had fallen in other parts of the country, mainly along the coastline, possibly intended for troops manning the coastal defences.

Once picked up or disturbed, they exploded. Children and others had been maimed. Due to the extended wings they caught up in trees or hung from other obstacles. They were the subject of curiosity until their deadly intent became well known.

Fortunately they were rare and not dropped in any great numbers. At one time there was a rumour that some had been found in our locality, but this was never confirmed and it was probably one of the many stories that did the rounds.

By then, we were very aware of the danger and mindful of the constant warnings 'Don't touch, or poke them with a stick'.

A particularly tragic incident occurred one Saturday morning in an Ealing shopping centre. The details were very vague then and I suspect have remained so. Information was suppressed at the time, but the customary 'Grapevine' among shop customers and the like, gradually pieced together a likely story.

Evidently, overnight a bomb had fallen in an alley alongside a small departmental store. This was declared a UXB and was due for excavation and disposal later in the day.

For some quite extraordinary reason, the shops were allowed to open for business as usual.

In mid-morning, with the area crowded with shoppers, it exploded, causing many casualties. It was obviously fitted with one of the deadly delayed action fuses.

I well remember the anger and criticism directed at the authorities and in particular, the unknown individual who made such a terrible and tragic error of judgement. The site is now occupied by a supermarket.

Ironically, just a few weeks after the spy saga, a bomb landed in the dead centre of the road virtually outside the suspect house. Again, a huge crater was ripped out that encroached across the pavements but caused little structural damage apart from windows and roof slates. To this day, those houses remain as neat and tidy terrace dwellings.

However, this one did create contingent problems, as it fractured all the service facilities including the water main. Water gushed out to rapidly fill the crater and overflow into the adjacent houses before the water could be turned off.

We now began to realise that an ominous pattern was developing. Virtually all the bombs in our immediate locality to date, had landed close, either side of the underground railway.

Could it be that from on high, this was being mistaken for a main line track?

As we lived virtually alongside, this was not a very consoling conclusion!

Thinking about it now, it was remarkable that 2 large calibre bombs had both struck the dead centre of the school road, either side of the rail bridge. Furthermore, that 2 others should land in the service road behind the next block of shops. Had there been a deviation of just 20 yards in any instance, then property destruction would have been widespread with undoubted casualties. As it was, we only heard of one lady cut by flying glass. She had just 'popped' indoors to make a cup of tea. Everyone else was sheltering somewhere.

Local archive records indicate that over 600 residential homes were destroyed and thousands damaged in what was then the borough of Ealing. The famous Ealing Film Studios were badly damaged but continued to produce morale boosting films and official documentaries. In November 1940, St Saviour's Church nearby was gutted by an incendiary bomb.

My mother's favourite shops were Jones and Knights and Abernethie's in West Ealing. My school clothes always came from the latter. Off she went on a shopping expedition to find some darning wool or sewing thread, which were both scarce. Evidently the local small shops had nothing left.

Mum returned fairly quickly and I can still picture her standing in our shop doorway with a shocked look on her face.

"What a mess" she said. "There's been a parachute mine up there. Lot of casualties they reckon. I couldn't get anywhere near the shops". As she came in she muttered "Bloody Jerries, I'm sick of it all". – Did my mother say that? Things really are getting serious!

THE MORNING AFTER THE NIGHT BEFORE
DECEMBER 1940 PARACHUTE MINE FELL BETWEEN BROUGHTON
ROAD AND HARTINGTON ROAD WEST EALING

It could well have been on that shopping trip that mum did find a bottle of banana essence, an essential ingredient of a recent recipe issued by the 'Ministry of Food' with the customary spiel 'It will do you good'.

Take half a national loaf, mash it up with parsnips, a pinch of sugar, then churn it all up with a few drips of the banana essence. Cook it gently in the oven and with a bit of luck out came something resembling 'Banana crumble'.

We were not impressed, how about trying it with marrows!

A far more edible and tasty dish was carrot croquettes. I have no idea of the specific ingredients but do know that cornflour featured. Only because I thought that mum had to use garden flowers!

The end result was fried in sausage shapes usually served with scrambled powdered egg.

Limited supplies of 'Spam' were now arriving from America. This was a real bonus of tasty meat substitute to enliven the drab menu that we had become used to.

'Woolton Pie' was the next masterpiece advertised in the newspapers and on posters. Don't tell us 'It will blah blah'.

This proved to be a disagreable concoction of potatoes, parsnips and herbs that justifiably became something of a wartime joke. In fact, mum used it as a form of threat if we upset her. "Woolton for dinner tonight if you are not careful".

We didn't actually starve, but ate some very peculiar things.

The daylight hours were now becoming a little more peaceful. The sirens were sounding less frequently and consequently school lessons were resuming an air of some normality. What a shame! After their mauling in the daylight attacks the Germans settled for the much less costly night raids. London continued to bear the brunt.

More home comforts were added to the shelter, including a dart board, but the main recreation continued to be the wireless. Although it was officially forbidden, people did tune in to listen to the infamous

'Lord Haw Haw', the alias of the British traitor William Joyce who broadcast from Hamburg.

This was not a question of being unpatriotic. We could not comprehend there being even one traitor, but simply that these nightly broadcasts provided a better laugh than some of the comedy programmes. His 'plum in the mouth' accent as he introduced himself 'Gairmany calling, Gairmany calling' always raised a chuckle and mimic.

The lying propaganda that followed was often quite ludicrous. I believe it is true to say that he announced on four separate occasions that the Aircraft Carrier Ark Royal had been sunk. Obviously a very resilient vessel!

Ironically, when this became fact, the B.B.C announced the sad news first.

On one occasion, cries of "Shush – Be quiet" echoed around the shelter as he announced that "Ealing, Queen of the London suburbs where so many wealthy landowners live, has been totally devastated by our glorious Luftwaffe".

An ironical cheer went up. As someone said "Great! If they reckon there is bugger all left they will leave us alone".

The night raids were now becoming a little more intermittent and we were even enjoying the odd luxury of a quiet night's sleep, but one evening the warning went quite early.

It must have been around tea time, as mum was preparing scrambled dried egg. This was the Friday night treat. Mum suggested that I took this down to the shelter where our clients were already assembling, spurred on by the 'early call'.

Mum said "I'll be down shortly, just got to tidy up and finish making dad's sandwiches for later".

Dad was already out and about. Sister Ivy was staying at work in Acton as she was on firewatch duty that night. Arthur was also on duty on his Thames firefloat.

Having finished my tea and chatting to the shelterers, aircraft could be heard overhead. This was routine and no cause for extraordinary alarm.

Suddenly, we could hear my mother yelling and shouting from above. It was difficult to comprehend what all the excited agitation was about, but obviously it was not dad's sandwiches!

As we raced up the cellar steps mum flung open the door and breathlessly gasped "Incendiary – Incendiary. It's in the garden".

Oh dear! So this was to be the moment of truth that I had trained for, excitedly awaited, yet secretly feared. Don't let mum down now.

I grabbed the dustbin lid, spare tin hat and the water bucket. Mum already had the stirrup pump ready. "It's out the back. I heard it land. Please God it's not near the tanks".

We eased open the back door. The incandescent glare was intense, but thankfully to our left, away from the Paraffin tanks.

With the dustbin lid in front of my face I edged out and by careful peeping around the edge of the lid was able to discern the location of the spitting fizzing device that was spraying out a shower of blazing magnesium droplets in a fiery hailstorm.

I was scared stiff, but had to be 'the man'. Mum constantly implored me to "Be careful, keep the lid up". I needed no bidding, having already adopted the training approach on knees and elbows. "Get lower" said mum. Any lower and I would be underground! It was now evident that this had fallen in the vegetable plot. Relatively safe, but the garden fence was already ablaze, only about 12 yards from the tanks. Problem – what do I tackle first?

A blaze of any sort was bad news, it tended to attract attention from above! Mum was now working away with the stirrup pump and I directed the first jet at the burning fence nearest the oil tanks. It would not go out. The magnesium was sticking like glue and immediately re-igniting after drenching.

Change to fine spray to obliterate the air supply, that's what the instructor said. Wow!, it worked.

Leave the fence now, have a go at the bomb. My mind was in a whirl but somehow worked things out. Hold the spray directly over the top of it. Suffocate the base of the fire. Hold it steady for as long as possible.

The spray faded and the device flared back to life. We needed more water quickly. The bucket was empty and I yelled out "More bloody water!"

Our cries had brought one of the ladies up from the cellar who began to replenish the bucket with the sink washing-up bowl. The faster she worked the more she sloshed about and missed the bucket.

The infernal thing was flaring again. Come on lady, move yourself!

I had a sudden thought. Oh God, don't let it have one of those explosive charges in it. Would it have gone off by now? What did they say at lectures? Was it at the beginning or towards the end of ignition – I must pay more attention but a bit late now!

We yelled at the bucket lady to grab one of the dirt filled sandbags surrounding the oil tank outhouse and as soon as she could get near enough, dump it on the thing.

Gradually we realised that the glare was diminishing and the spitting dying down. We could be winning. Elation now replaced fear, just keep that water coming.

Right, we've done it! Chuck that sandbag on now. She missed! Get another one quick. Good shot. From beneath the bag came a last desparing splutter and fizzle. Gotcha!

I changed back to jet and hosed down the fence until the last vestige of flame and glow disappeared..

All the gear was collected and we had a final check round. Must not forget to replenish the bucket.

Mum said "Why didn't we use the garden hose?" Good idea, but this would not have provided the essential fine spray. However, it would have replenished the bucket more efficiently. Another lesson learned.

"Right" said mum, "I reckon that deserves a cup of tea, but first get out of those wet clothes".

It was only then that I realised just how wet I was. Probably the sweat of fear!

We returned to the shelter where I was greeted as something of a hero. Just wait until the others get home to hear all about it. I reckoned that fireman Arthur would be well impressed.

It was much later that evening when mother pulled me to one side and said quietly, "I'd rather you didn't use that word bloody, it's not very nice you know".

Midst all that drama and excitement my mother's sense of propriety did not falter!

Whilst the majority of my wartime souvenirs were thrown away I did keep the tail fins of this incendiary bomb.

Now attached to a 'mock' base the model is used for educational purposes at our local Gunnersbury Park Museum.

School children studying World War 2 are fascinated to learn of its authentic history.

It must have been about that time when huge salvage drives were launched. Make do and mend was the order of the day in every respect.

Scrap material of every sort was collected, from rags to bones. Cloth was re-pulped and the bones were used to extract glue for aircraft frames.

Gangs of workmen toured the streets with blow torches removing ornamental iron railings from parks and front garden walls. Many squabbles ensued when it came to the garden gate, but they had to go.

The story was, that all this iron would be melted down to make tanks and ships.

Long after the war it was revealed that massive piles of rusting metal were hidden away in the countryside. The primary object of the exercise seems to have been to make people feel that they had made a positive material contribution to the war effort.

Rather surprisingly, I could still get my favourite comics, the Beano and Hotspur. A bit thinner perhaps and the stories all had a war theme, usually making fun of the Axis leaders.

Mussolini, due to his large girth, was always good for a laugh. 'Musso da Wop, he's a big-a-de-flop . He gave his troops Spaghetti for bootlaces!

It was not all juvenile humour however, there were serious articles on the theme of 'Our wonderful fighting men' and 'How you can do your bit'.

Even now, I can remember the words of a catchy little tune we used to sing, again poking fun at the enemy. To the tune of the dwarfs working song in Disney's Snow White, it went,

"Whistle while you work, Hitler is a twerp. Goerings barmy, so's his army, whistle while you work."

Another bomb fell a little too close for comfort. No more than 30 yards away, but fortunately this was of smaller calibre.

Once again, this fell in the same alley type access road behind the next block of shops.

This one also burrowed deeply into the soft earth beneath the gravel surface before exploding.

In the cellar, we felt the thud and earth tremor, but assumed that it was some distance away, whereas in the long term it proved to be the closest.

This was another example whereby the blast effect was nullified by the depth of the detonation, but it did rip out an impressive crater. A few windows were broken, but the most spectacular effect was that the surrounding buildings were smothered with clinging lumps of wet clay and earth, like barnacles on the hull of a ship.

The minimal effect of spread blast on this occasion was graphically illustrated by the greengrocer's delivery bike still leaning nonchalantly against the fence where it had been left overnight no more than 25 yards from the crater edge!

The only major problem was a fractured water main which spewed a geyser high into the air.

Compared to others, this was a 'Doddle'. The pipe was repaired, crater filled in and gravel spread. Within two days little remained to remind us of the incident, as the greengrocer's boy resumed his deliveries on the 'lucky' bike.

Another so-called luxury was installed in the shelter. A wind-up gramophone which played 78 rpm records. The sound was reproduced through steel needles accompanied by a frying fat sound as the needles wore down.

It was very much a case of 'What you hear is what you get'. There was no chance of being able to purchase either new needles or records. The repetition of a limited selection of music drove everyone mad and the infernal machine was destined for a brief inglorious life.

Brother Bern's fiancée Joyce travelled all over the country, camping out or staying in bed and breakfast accommodation to be near to him as he moved around.

During one such journey Joyce was on a train heading out of London at the height of a raid. They had not travelled very far when the train halted. Bombs were falling all around and all hell was let loose outside as the passengers, mainly service personnel, awaited some instruction, possibly to evacuate the train.

Passengers were very carefully peeping out of the carriage black-out blinds. To her dismay, Joyce realised that they had stopped directly opposite a well known match factory.

What a place to be stranded! She thought 'If they 'strike' that we could be in bother!'

The minutes ticked by, still no advice, when suddenly, 'Whoof' as a bomb hit the factory.

Discipline and decorum went out of the window, as did all the passengers!

They opted for the long drop down to the track on the opposite side of the carriages, then sprinted away across the other rails to get as far away as possible before another seemingly inevitable 'big bang'.

Somehow, by walking and I believe a taxi part way, Joyce made it back to our house in the early hours, very tired and dishevelled. Future Daughter-in-law or not, my mother had a few choice words to say.

It did not make the slightest difference. Joyce continued to follow Bern around until he was posted overseas. Mum commented "Good job you won't know where he is going, you would be off there as well!"

It was inevitable that Bern would be sent overseas before long, but when it did happen it was very sudden, with only 5 days embarkation leave.

They decided to get married and rushed around to get a special license.

This was to be my first experience of a wedding. It sounded like an interesting diversion until they threatened to make me a page boy in a velvet suit. No way!

Thankfully they were kidding me.

Obviously, wartime marriages were very austere occasions.

A registry office ceremony followed by whatever reception ingenuity could conjure up. Except for one significant feature I cannot recall exactly what my mother achieved for the buffet, but am sure that it was a miracle akin to the parable of the loaves and fishes. However, there was an impressive looking wedding cake. A two tier arrangement that looked the part, except that the base portion was a cardboard 'look-alike' with fake fancy icing and the small top tier was sponge cake.

I did not go to the ceremony, being detailed to stay at home to look after things. What a silly idea! Here was I, a ten year old lad deprived of any goodies for a long time, confronted with a table full of interesting bits and pieces.

This must go down as one of my more memorable escapades. To this day I have no idea where or how mum acquired a tin of cheese straws. Even pre-war these would have been a luxury item.

I thought, now these look interesting. Wonder what they taste like? Surely they won't miss a couple. Oh yes, very tasty. One more won't hurt, or another. I just could not resist the temptation and carried on until the tin was half empty. Panic, I could be in big trouble this time.

The few guests were tucking in when mum decided to hand the tin around, which changed my immediate life dramatically!

My pathetic excuse that the cat had eaten them only made matters worse.

I still have a taste for cheese straws and they never fail to remind me of that occasion. My pocket money was stopped for a while until I pointed out that this was prejudicial to the war effort. People were exhorted to save money, as well as everything else.

National savings were boosted by groups and of course at school. Savers were encouraged by the publication of price lists, showing for example, that a bomb could be made for £100 and a mere incendiary for 15 shillings. At current prices this sounds more like a firework for November the 5th!

As mentioned earlier, London was festooned with Barrage Balloons floating in the sky like bloated whales. Each was moored to the back of a lorry by a winch arrangement – well, most of the time! The steel cables were designed to prevent low level attacks on important buildings or facilities.

Very occasionally in bad weather one of the monsters would escape its tether to create mayhem as it roamed around.

I could hear all the excitement in the shop and dashed out in time to see a rogue balloon gusting along above our road trailing cables that were snagging the rooftops. As it reached the houses opposite, one of the cables neatly decapitated the cluster of chimney pots which came crashing down, bringing with them shattered roof slates. Seemingly pleased with that mischief the balloon rose up again and set off in the direction of London.

The lady of the house came running out complaining bitterly. Several rooms were smothered in soot and debris, quite apart from the holes in her roof. As usual, mum went to the rescue to help out with the cleaning up, whilst dad contacted the emergency services to provide temporary tarpaulin sheets for the roof.

The 'Blitz' on London raged on from September 1940 through to May 1941 with almost continual attacks by night.

Following this, there were periods of lull, but never a moment when vigilance could be relaxed. Post war records indicate that raids continued for 57 consecutive nights through to November 2nd and regularly thereafter, but with decreasing frequency and intensity. However, on specific occasions the respite was savagely shattered. On the nights of April 16th and 19th 1941, vast fleets of 700 bombers unleashed their deadly cargoes all over the capital. Then, on May 10th in bright moonlight, 500 aircraft dropped 700 tons of high explosives and 7000 canisters of incendiaries. Some 2000 separate fires were created.

In the aftermath of this raid, one third of London streets were impassable and many famous buildings damaged, including the Royal Mint – House of Commons – Tower of London and the Law Courts.

A further 1400 civilians were killed.

From then on, occasional, but still serious raids were made for virtually the duration of the war, culminating in the launch of Hitler's secret 'V' weapons in June 1944, just one week after the Allied 'D Day' invasion of Europe.

At home, we certainly enjoyed the blessed relief of firstly the odd peaceful night which gradually extended as the weeks went by into the summer of 1941.

Ultimately, the 'Blitz' on London killed 32.000 people, What a terrible price to pay.

Whenever I think of my father, it is with a 'fag' in his hand or mouth. In those days cigarettes were a great personal solace. Smoking was widespread and actually encouraged as 'stress relief'. No councillors to chat to! This was of course long before the health hazards perceived today.

Non smokers were in the minority. Cigarette prices were low, about 10 pence (4 pence today) for 10. Dad smoked a revolting brand called 'Tenners'. We reckoned that they were made from camel dung. I suppose that in those days they could well have been!

On my eleventh birthday in June 1941 I moved up to the 'Big Boys' school. Somehow mum had scraped together sufficient clothing coupons to get me the required social distinction of long trousers. I was a proud but self conscious lad who ventured out for the first time in them. 'I'm a man!

By now I could be more help to dad with his caretaking duties, even stoking the huge boilers with coke to simmer overnight. Not one of my favourite jobs. It was hard work.

Pumping out water from the shelters lost its appeal once the warmer weather arrived. No more skating rinks.

Talking about the shelters reminds me of the occasion that dad brought home a nice fat marrow. There was a flaw on the surface skin, but nothing out of the ordinary – until mum cut it open. Inside was a large lump of anti-aircraft shell shrapnel! This must have fallen when the marrow was small, which had then grown around it. Mum said "I've heard of iron rations, but this is ridiculous!"

Food was a never ending worry and problem. An everlasting test of ingenuity. Fish was rare, but a welcome variation. It was later in the war, perhaps 1944, but I recall a lady running into the shop to tip off mum that a delivery was being made to the fishmonger. The inevitable queue was already forming.

As usual, dad was missing somewhere. "That man is never around when needed" exclaimed mum. With no further ado, she shut up the shop and scurried off to join the rapidly lengthening queue, with the hopeful prospect of maybe one fish, whatever the 'breed'. However, today was different. The first introduction of Whale meat! 'Goodness me' thought mum. 'If the allowance is one each today, I'm going to need a bigger shopping basket!'

This proved to be something really different. We examined the chunky steak like object with suspicion and sniffed its oily aroma.

If the cooked end result did not show a vast improvement, then Stripey the cat would think it was his birthday.

As always, mum was equal to the challenge. Advice had been given regarding the method of cooking and I vaguely remember that by gently warming in the oven first, much of the oil content could be drained away to leave an edible looking chunk of meat. This could be fried or roasted and was actually quite tasty. A meal could be concocted for say evening, with chips, or a main dinner with roast potatoes. As always, marrow would supplement the vegetables.

A while later, tinned Barracuda found its way into shops, disguised under the wierd name of 'Snoek'. Presumably to ensure that no-one had the faintest idea what they were eating.

In June 1941 Hitler made a grave error of judgement by attacking Russia. The British people could now be confident that the threat of invasion had passed. Also, with the Luftwaffe preoccupied elsewhere, may we dare hope that London would be permitted to resume an air of normality?

The propaganda slogan 'London Can Take It' now rang true. The populace had endured great losses and privations with tremendous courage and true grit.

It was soon evident that the authorities shared this optimism as bomb sites were being cleared up and restoration of damaged buildings began in earnest. Our shop and house received the treatment and it was so nice to see sunshine through the windows again after many months of gloom. I had the task of taping up all the glass again. As mum said, "Don't want to tempt providence".

The academic aspect of my life now adopted more importance. Lessons resumed a more orderly routine and I was progressing through the Senior school, class by class. In those days there were up to 40 pupils in each class and 'your' teacher took most subjects, except for the more specialised such as carpentry, music or games. The latter took place in the playground, as all open spaces were used for more useful purposes. Each appropriate term, one would move up a class according to your birth date.

I was not at that stage a very accomplished pupil. I quite enjoyed English and Geography, but Arithmetic, Ugh! I hated it.

This was well reflected by my marks. Overall, I guess that I was an average, could do better character.

A new innovation at school was the appearance of metal bins entitled 'Pig Swill'. Were they starting school dinners we wondered!

The idea was, that kids brought from home all the left-overs such as potato peelings, pea shucks and the like. In my case, marrow peel! Despite daily collections, in the summer months they did tend to 'pong' a bit.

Carpentry became one of my favoured subjects, obviously influenced by the talent of brother Ted.

The teacher, a Mr Lepley, was an elderly but kind patient man who had a unique method of maintaining discipline. He accomplished deadly accuracy with a chunk of semi-hard rubber he called Oscar. Misbehave or mess about and 'Thwack'. Oscar would catch you somewhere about the head. I wonder what the present day 'Children's Act' or whatever, would make of that!

With the lull now allowing more freedom of movement, I began to visit my brother's wife Betty who lived at Northolt, just a couple of miles from the R.A.F station which had played such a major role in the Battle of Britain. With Ted away, Betty found it hard to cope with the loneliness. They had a nice bungalow purchased in 1939 for the princely sum of £950.

Betty had one of the indoor shelters, known as the Morrison, named after Herbert Morrison the Minister of Home Security. This was a tough structure about the size of a large dining table, with a thick steel top and bolted metal legs. Thick wire mesh sides could be hooked in place to prevent rubble falling in. The great advantage was, that it could be used as a dining table during the day and sleep a family of four at night. It was a tight squeeze, and you had to be good friends!

These were distributed free to low income families and over half a million were supplied in the first year of war.

We took a stroll most days, invariably down to the airfield to watch the activity. At intervals on the route we would look with interest at large hangar-type structures alongside the main road. These were artistically painted to resemble houses, complete with windows and curtains.

One could make a good guess, but we were never really sure what these contained. Until one day as we passed by, the fuselage of a Spitfire was being towed out. It was subsequently learned that most contained such major components or spare parts.

Our 'walkabouts' did in fact cause Betty some embarrassment. By now I was quite a tall lad, resplendent in my long trousers. This gave rise to a spate of whispered gossip around the neighbours. Betty was seeing another man – and he was staying overnight!

Earlier on, the 'Free Polish' squadrons were based at Northolt. They had displayed magnificent courage once they were made operational at a critical stage of the battle in 1940.

The impressive memorial and gardens that now stand alongside the major trunk road past the airfield is not only a fitting tribute to their courage, but a constant reminder provided by mention of the location 'The Polish War Memorial' in traffic reports, road maps and the like.

One day, as we stood watching the 'planes coming and going, we became aware of frantic activity developing on the field with rescue vehicles rushing out to line the runway. In the far distance we could discern a twin engined aircraft laboriously making a way in with smoke pouring from one engine.

We could now hear the discordant roar as the single engine was coaxed by the pilot to maintain height.

It certainly looked far too low. Oh God, would they make it? We stood transfixed with trembling apprehension as it neared the row of houses just beyond the airfield boundary.

Slowly the stricken 'plane came nearer and lower. It's not going to make it!

We could hardly bear to watch, but were willing it on with all our heart and mind. Just above the rooftops it clipped a chimney stack and faltered, but with a last desparing burst of power the aircraft staggered on to 'Belly flop' onto the end of the runway in a skidding, slewing cloud of dust and debris.

What a relief! We were some distance away, but as the emergency vehicles raced in we were able to see the crew jumping out and sprinting away from the wreck. What a brilliant achievement by that pilot.

Betty and myself were shattered by the tension. It defies imagination what it must have been like for the crew.

R.A.F fire appliances sprayed foam all over the aircraft until it resembled a giant soufflé.

As we wended our way home we just could not get the nerve tingling drama out of our mind. The images have certainly remained with me and every time that I pass Northolt I can still picture the scene.

Following the Luftwaffe attacks on R.A.F airfields in the early stages of the 'Battle of Britain in 1940, Northolt was attacked on several occasions but with little damage. Less than 20 bombs actually struck the base, some harmlessly, but a large number fell in residential areas near to the base during a raid by 6 aircraft in September 1940.

It was estimated that over 100 bombs, mainly the smaller 50kg type straddled the Greenford region about 2 miles short of the base. How on earth they missed such a vast target is beyond comprehension. Once again, it was civilians who suffered. Several hundred houses were destroyed or damaged and 37 people killed.

It was fortunate that a number of bombs failed to explode.

As a sequel to this episode I must now 'fast forward' to 1981. During my National Service in the R.A.F I undertook a bomb disposal course and thereby became familiar with WW2 weapons. Subsequently, as founder and eventually president of a local football club we had our ground in Greenford about 2 miles from the airfield.

This was always being developed and during some excavation work we dug up what appeared to be the tail fins of a small bomb.

Apart from the thought 'Wonder where the rest of it is', it was forgotten until the day that with a colleague, we were digging out a small drainage ditch. This was on a Saturday morning prior to an important league game.

Working alongside a public footpath my mate's spade clanged onto a solid metal object. Hopping around muttering expletives and massaging his wrist I was devoid of sympathy and merely said "Don't be a Jessie, get on with it – it's only a bomb".

Moments later he said "Hey Roy, what do you reckon this is?".

I looked with increasing apprehension as he scraped away more soil to reveal a cylindrical shape that seemed awfully familiar, with all the characteristics of a German 50kg fragmentation bomb. The very type that would have been used against airfields.

This was now serious. As we gingerly lifted the heavy object I said something like "What I don't want to find is a hexagonal cap somewhere about here". Feeling around underneath I froze as my fingers located such a large nut.

Right – that's it! What do we do now? With the important football in a few hours and with the philosophy that it had lain happily for 41 years, so another few hours wouldn't matter, we covered it with a sheet of wood and kept quiet!

As it happened, the referee that afternoon was a police inspector so I decided to tell him after the game.

His face was a picture. A mixture of apprehension and disbelief. I think he was more upset that he had promised to take his wife out that evening, but was now 'lumbered' to take temporary charge of the 'incident'.

A few phone calls and it was all happening. A 'Posse' of police descended to seal off the footpath and to move nearby residents to the front of their houses with a warning not to look out of their rear windows.

It was amusing to me to see policemen walking past the object on tiptoe and talking in whispers.

A police 'Big boss' with a fancy hat approached me and said "Would you mind guarding it? – We are keeping everyone else at a safe distance". Thanks very much, I like you too!

He went on to say that they had contacted the army bomb disposal depot at Hounslow who were on their way.

It was now getting dark. I felt lonely and getting colder by the minute. I could do with a cup of tea – and a wee!

Back in the nice warm clubhouse most people thought it funny, a bit of a hoax, but my wife was very worried and in a right flap.

Time went by. It had all gone quiet except for the constant hum of traffic along the Western Avenue. It was over an hour later when a young man arrived in civilian clothes. He had been 'Bleeped' whilst out shopping with his wife in Hounslow.

"Hi there, so what have we got?" he asked.

I explained the circumstances and the probable legacy of the raids on Northolt base during the war. Also, that some months earlier we had found bomb tail fins in another part of the ground.

As we stood chatting with this grey rusting object for company, I realised that this chap did not have a clue. Little knowledge of WW2 and amazed to learn that Northolt had actually been attacked! He finally admitted that he specialised in modern devices and had never even seen a conventional bomb.

Not what I would call a very encouraging start!

He went back to his car and returned with a case full of instruments. "I can only do my best" he muttered, pulling out what appeared to be a doctor's stethoscope with a probe thing on the end.

"Would you help me please – Lift the end up a bit more"

The 'Blunt' end was open and exposed, presumably where the tail fins had been torn off on impact. There seemed to be a small tube down the middle of the casing, but this looked very fragile.

So there was I, sitting on the damp ground with a suspect bomb between my legs. My new friend said "Hold it steady, I'm going to insert this probe up the rear end". – Pardon? – Oh, I see. My eyes had started to water!

Very carefully and slowly the probe made its way through 40 odd years of silt in the tube. With the stethoscope in his ears his face was a picture of concentration. I was not sure what he expected to hear but mentioned that if he heard ticking, would he kindly let me know! He replied "Sure will. If you can catch me up!"

At the end of all this fiddling about he concluded that the object was sinister, but would require the expertise of the specialist bomb squad based at Chatham. Alternatively, he could arrange for it to be 'Blown' on site. No way! You are not going to blow a ruddy great hole in my football pitch.

He chatted on the phone to the officer in charge at Chatham, who responded immediately, travelling with a police motor cycle escort.

In the meantime the situation was being reported on the evening TV news broadcasts.

Muggins was again left to guard the thing, but I did sneak off for a cup of tea and some warm clothing.

It was not until 9pm that a vehicle arrived with 3 uniformed army bomb squad officers. More police and a fire appliance were now in attendance.

The boss man said "What are you doing here?" – "Er, guarding it". We had a chat and then I was told to get lost. Duty done.

It was almost midnight before they eventually lifted the object onto a rubber clad cradle and drove slowly out of the gate. We found out from a newspaper reporter that it was blown up out on the Romney Marshes.

On reflection, I have had better days. We lost the game as well!

Reverting back to 1940, my brother Bern had disappeared overseas. We had no news for quite a while, but eventually learned that he had been seconded to the 'West African Rifles', stationed in what was then known as the Gold Coast. It was a consolation to us, that so far this had been a quiet sector of the world-wide conflict.

He had been promoted to the exulted rank of Regimental Sergeant Major and was in charge of the vehicle repair workshops.

My parents commented in some disbelief "Good gracious. That boy a Sergeant Major!"

Poor Bern, his carefree attitude to life made him akin to the 'Black sheep' of the family, however unjustly.

He wrote to me describing life in Africa. The heat and strange customs. Always good for a laugh, he described a telephone conversation with an African worker who answered "Who dat". Bern replied "Who dat". This exchange continued until the voice at the other end exclaimed "Who dat who say who dat when I say who dat!"

This character eventually became very loyal to my brother and when the time came for Bern to leave Africa he clung to him sobbing uncontrollably. The only problem was, that he ran onto the parade ground in full view of all the assembled men.

Can you imagine anything more embarrassing for a Regimental Sergeant Major?

Meanwhile, elder brother Ted was stationed in Norfolk, but would not tell us what he was doing. Any enquiry was brushed aside, "Oh, nothing much". It was much later that we learned that he was engaged on airfield defence with a new fangled secret weapon. Basically, rockets were fired into the air with cables trailing. These were aimed in the path of low flying aircraft.

After the war Ted admitted that he never did fire them in anger, or heard of any other success. It probably seemed to be a good idea at the time, or perhaps had been invented too late. Something like this may well have proved effective in the early stages when the Luftwaffe were straffing the R.A.F airfields.

All our family letters concluded with a 'Gang sign'. A little matchstick man with one hand to his head, fingers encircling one eye. We tried to outdo each other with the funniest caption.

A national variation to this theme was a caricature of a bald domed head and protruding nose peeking over a wall. This little fellow was known as 'Chad' and appeared on posters captioned with an apt conclusion to the words 'Wot – No.....'

As mentioned earlier, night raids were now spasmodic and nothing like the intensity of the winter months, but of course, one had to occur when I was staying with Betty.

It proved to be quite heavy and we cowered under the Morrison shelter, listening with apprehension as aircraft droned overhead. We could hear the occasional 'crump' of bombs. Were they having another go at the airfield? This was unusual by night, but equally strange that without a specific target, the enemy aircraft had ventured so far West of London.

We shall never know the answer. The raid was fairly brief and when the All-clear sounded, we peered out of the front door towards the airfield. A fire was visible, but well away from that region.

Turning to the back, two more fires could be seen in the distance towards Ealing. Few people had private telephones in those days so there was no opportunity of gaining mutual assurance by contacting my parents.

On my train journey home next morning, a row of houses alongside the track had been reduced to rubble and the rescue services were still swarming over the debris searching for victims.

It is fair to say that mum was pleased to see me! It was a long time before I resumed such jaunts. "She can stay lonely" said mum.

As the warm summer of 1941 merged into Autumn, the war was not going well. In Russia, the German armies had reached Kiev and were poised to threaten Moscow. Earlier we had relished the pursuit and destruction of the German Battleship Bismark by the Royal Navy, but this was nullified by our loss of the fine Battleship Hood. A single unlucky shell penetrated the stern magazine and she blew-up with only 3 survivors.

Our armies in North Africa were vainly battling to relieve the surrounded garrison of Tobruk. The Mediterranean island of Crete had been lost. Malta was under seige by continual air bombardment. Would we ever get any good news?

The evenings were now drawing in again. We wondered, would this bring any resumption of the nightly raids.

On November 11th, the Aircraft Carrier Ark Royal was torpedoed in the Mediterranean. Lord Haw Haw's vivid imagination was now sadly true.

All was not well and for the first time an air of despondency became apparant, but thankfully no evidence of a 'Blitz' resumption.

In early December, all single women between the ages of 20 to 30 were called up for the services or directed to work of national importance such as the 'Land Army'.

We lost one of our most popular lady teachers who joined the WAAFs.

Dad's caretaking duties took on a new dimension when he became one of the first 'Children Crossing' attendants, resplendent in a white coat and carrying a 'Stop' sign, made up in the woodwork centre. He patrolled a main road crossing adjacent to the school. My wife Beryl, will always remember 'Pop' as he was known, ushering her across to attend the same school, but a couple of years behind me. I guess that this sideline earned dad an extra couple of bob.

Ironically, whilst I did not know Beryl at that time, and would not have spoken to such a little girl kid anyway, I did have a crush on her elder sister Joyce who was in my mixed class.

We used to pass little cashew sweets with love messages on them across the class. It was not until many years later that we realised who was who and our 'sweet' affair was revealed.

On December 7th 1941, Japan attacked the American fleet at Pearl Harbour. School Geography took on a new dimension, adding the Far East to our education.

On the 11th, Germany and Italy also declared war on the United States, which took immediate reciprocal action.

After standing totally alone for 18 long months, Britain had at last a powerful ally, but equally another formidable adversary. This was immediately emphasised when news came that we had lost the Battleship 'Prince of Wales' and the Battle Cruiser 'Repulse', both sunk by Japanese aircraft in the Indian Ocean.

Christmas Day that year was very drab. Every aspect of life was grim and I am unable to recall any joyous moment, not even a present of note. Indeed, that very evening it was announced that the British garrison at Hong Kong had been forced to surrender. 'Merry Christmas' was not a popular expression and 'Happy New Year' an even more forlorn hope.

By now, I was able to help out with customer deliveries using the heavy old iron bike with fixed panniers at the back and front. Until then I could hardly lift the thing, let alone ride it. This gave me a little more pocket money by way of tips as I delivered cans of Paraffin, logs, and other domestic items. That is, until I fell off! This monster had a mind of its own and I reckon it threw me off!

It was a definite indication that I was growing up when my mother expressed more concern at the state of my trousers than my welfare. Understandable I guess. Apparantly we had no clothing coupons left, so it was another patch up job.

In 1942, the first American servicemen arrived in Britain.

We began to hear all sorts of stories about these smart well dressed fellows with plenty of money in their pockets. We had not yet seen any around Ealing, but there was always a customer who knew someone who knew someone who knew one.

The stories grew wilder every day. Did we know that they had an aircraft called a Flying Fortress that could drop a bomb down a pickle barrel from 20.000 feet. We all wondered why anyone would want to bomb a pickle barrel anyway!

Then, late one afternoon, into the shop strolled two smartly uniformed young men, greeting dad with a drawled "Hi Pop, how you doin"? Although taken aback by the unaccustomed familiarity, dad responded "Good afternoon sir. Can I help you?".

Mum quickly appeared from the back of the shop determined not to miss anything. "Well hello mam, you look just like my mom back home", which threw her into a tizzy of embarrassment.

The chat flowed easily and dad was completely won over by the gift of a packet of 'Lucky Strike' cigarettes.

They were full of questions about the 'Blitz', as it was still evident that the area had suffered, despite the big clear-up.

It was my good fortune that I arrived home from school midst all this chat. "Hey, who's the young fella" they exclaimed. Wow! so this was the Yanks.

All the kids at school had been practicing the recommended greeting, 'Got any gum chum', but I was too shy to try this out. One of them came from Texas, so I asked if he was a Cowboy. It may seem strange now, but none of us had ever met an American in our lives.

Newly arrived, they were based in Bushy Park near Richmond and had taken a bus ride to see the sights. Ealing was going to be something of a let down!

Mum offered them a cup of tea, something of a novelty for them, but they enjoyed it, or so they said.

We explained the location of Ealing to central London and with the underground station next door they were delighted to be pointed in the right direction for some action, as they called it.

Thinking about it, I am not sure whether they actually bought anything, but who cared. They were like a breath of fresh air.

As they were leaving, one said "Hey kiddo, would you like some candy". Candy?, what's that? I'd rather have some sweets I thought, then gasped as he handed me a whole bar of chocolate and a packet of chewing gum.

I had almost forgotten what chocolate tasted like. This was a treasure indeed.

Mum immediately confiscated the bar to be rationed out, knowing full well that given half a chance I would have scoffed the lot in one go.

All that reminds me of an amusing incident that occurred quite recently.

Our local Gunnersbury Park Museum arrange very interesting 'Period Costume' educational sessions for children, one of which depicts 'Life in the 1940s'.

I had the pleasure of taking part in one series to 10 year old students.

Having demonstrated gas masks, air raid shelters, food rationing and school life under air attack, the years moved on to 1942 and the arrival in Britain of hundreds of thousand American servicemen.

The lady teacher expounded the tremendous social impact that they introduced to the austerity of war weary Britain.

They had access to luxury goods, not seen or long forgotten, such as nylon stockings, chocolate bars, peanut butter, chewing gum, tinned meat and fruit etc.

Even on the music side there was a cultural revolution as we were introduced to jazz, swing bands, jukeboxes and the jitterbug.

Came question time and the teacher said "Now, can anyone suggest to me what other things the American servicemen may have introduced to Britain at that time?"

Up shot a little lad's hand – "Please miss, Babies!"

The senior school playground included a science and woodwork building which had a flat roof.

Games at break-time invariably ended when some clown lobbed the ball high onto the roof there to stay, unless my father could be persuaded to get the ladder out in his 'spare' time. No chance!.

Due to wartime shortages, rubber was a vital commodity, therefore no such things as balls were being made. The limited quantity that we had to kick-about was dwindling fast. Things were getting serious. Sweet talking dad failed miserably, he was just too busy.

I reckoned that if one of my mates would stay behind one evening to hold the ladder, we could get up there out of sight at the end of the building. If caught we would be in dead trouble, but it was worth a try.

We struggled with the heavy old wooden ladder which extended by means of rope pulleys, but finally got the thing against the wall. Making sure that dad was pre-occupied elsewhere I very nervously started the climb. My first time up a ladder, maybe dad will hear my knees knocking!

'Why didn't I keep my big mouth shut'. Rung by rung, boyish bravado and the unhelpful taunts of my so called mate spurred me on to thankfully clamber onto the roof.

Wow! What a bonanza. Balls of every description lay around and were tossed down with gay abandon. Until, what's that? Another object caught my eye. 'Oh no! – What do I do now?' There at my feet lay an unexploded incendiary bomb.

There was a deep indentation in the asphalt roof where this had landed, knocking off the tail fins.

First devilish thoughts were to toss this down to my mate "Catch!" but seriously, this was a real dilemma. Do I leave it and keep quiet, or come clean on the escapade?

Clutching the tail fins as a trophy I made a precarious way down.

We dithered about, but finally decided that we really had no choice but to accept the consequences and set off to find dad.

His reaction was not so bad. We suffered the inevitable lecture, "Supposing you had fallen and broken your neck. No good running to me" type, but his mind was more focussed on the device.

We reported to the wardens post in the school yard and as darkness fell a sergeant from the bomb disposal squad arrived. He packed the incendiary in a sand filled metal box and lowered this down from the roof. The school authorities remained in ignorance of this affair, it seemed prudent to forget it ever happened.

We did have another interesting diversion at home when for some obscure reason a twelve strong all-girl bagpipe band used our large upstairs lounge for a meeting. They were a touring group entertaining the troops. The only logic to the choice of our house was the proximity to the underground station. Evidently their next performance was in London.

My parents agreed, with the proviso that they did not play the things! I dashed home from school to find these mini kilted dollies tripping up and down the stairs. Coooor! - no wonder they entertained the troops. I wondered. Was it only Scottish men who wore nothing under a kilt? My fact finding mission was abruptly curtailed. "Roy, in here NOW" yelled mum. Consequently, all these years later I am none the wiser.

Mum was pleased to receive a tin of Highland Shortbread biscuits.

Oh! what a relief and joy to get some good news for a change. We were all glued to the wireless for every snippet of information as in October 1942, word came through that British and Commonwealth troops under the command of General Montgomery (Monty), had launched a massive attack from El Alemein in North Africa and after fierce fighting the German Africa Corps were in full retreat back across the Western desert. So, they are not invincible after all!

This was a tremendous boost to the folks at home. Winston Churchill ordered the church bells to be rung throughout the country for the first time since the threat of invasion in 1940.

Geography lessons took on an almost exciting aspect as we followed the campaign. Desert outposts with names such as Qattara, Matruh, Sidi Barrani and even Buq Buq, slipped off the tongue with ease as every day another village or town was captured with increasing rapidity. This proved to be a massive victory and a turning point in the war. When Allied forces landed in Algeria soon afterwards the retreating Axis army was trapped and ultimately surrendered in May 1943.

My teenage years were now beckoning. Things were relatively quiet with only occasional air raids to keep us on our toes. Everything was in short supply. Food rations reached an all time low, but there were glimmers of hope. The massive influx of American servicemen was having a positive effect to the austerity of Britain.

With access to luxury goods such as perfume, stockings, chocolate and cigarettes, the 'Yanks' were certainly a hit with the ladies. More importantly, American foodstuff began to appear in the shops to provide a welcome variation to the drab fare that we had become accustomed to. Officially, these goods were on points allocation, but before long there was always someone who knew a 'Yank'.

Reaching my final year at school I was surprised to be appointed a prefect, but more so to be made school vice-captain.

In that capacity I became one of the very first 'Lollipop' crossing attendants for an initial 6 month pilot scheme of childrens road safety. Obviously, my fathers initiative had caught someone's eye.

My father remained alone at the busy main road junction. With two colleagues I was detailed to patrol a crossroad at the other end of the school road. Thinking about it now, it must have been a nice easy job, there was hardly any traffic.

There was still the occasional daylight raid and the regulations were, that should the sirens sound whilst on the way to school, children ran home or to school, whichever was nearer. Guess what! To us kids home was always nearest, even from the school gate!

This was ably demonstrated one morning just before nine o'clock. We were on duty, now resplendent in black berets with a 'Firebrand' badge and carrying our 'STOP' boards.

The sirens sounded and immediately hundreds of kids poured out of the three schools and stampeded like a herd of cattle towards us. Faced with an instant decision of discipline or be trampled to death, we made a very courageous choice.

Lowering our boards sideways we stood resolutely in the middle of the road. Miraculously the rampaging horde slowed down and shuffled to a shambolic halt. Astonished and encouraged we yelled at them to line up in fours on the pavement and march smartly back to school.

To this day, I cannot believe the extraordinary response, which serves to emphasise the discipline of those days.

The look of utter incredibility on the face of the headmaster at the gate, was a joy to behold. We were only mere prefects after all.

Unknown to us, that very day the authorities were secretly observing the worth of these new fangled road safety patrols. The subsequent report should have made interesting reading!

I do therefore claim a significant contribution to the now familiar 'Lollipop' crossings.

We had become far too complacent. The shelter regulars had dwindled down to a few stalwarts and our family had returned to a nice warm bed in our own rooms.

Suddenly 'out of the blue' the Luftwaffe hit London again in March and April of 1944, in what was termed the 'Little Blitz'. Heavier and more powerful bombs were used than in the earlier raids, also a larger and more deadly incendiary device.

There was another twist, that instead of following the usual route straight up the river Thames, this time the raiders took a sweep around the capital and came in from the West. Through the back door one might say. Consequently the formations passed directly over our area.

As some compensation we now had vastly improved anti-aircraft defences, including a new invention – a rocket launcher.

These made the most infernal noise. Even if they missed, they would frighten the bomber crew to death!

There was a tremendous barrage of gunfire, but a downside was, that a fair number of shells failed to explode in the air, but did so on impact with the ground. Many incidents are recorded as A.A Shell damage, or UX shell.

This series of raids killed some 1500 people and injured 3000 more. It is reasonable to suppose that had the populace not been lulled into a false sense of security, such casualties would have been reduced.

In addition, the Germans kept up a day and night 'Hit and run' tactic against coastal towns and cities throughout England. Thankfully, this proved to be a fairly brief and concluding foray before the day of reckoning. The last Luftwaffe operation over the British Isles took place on April 10th 1945, just a few weeks before Germany capitulated.

I was now approaching my 14th birthday and leaving school at the end of term in July.

I really had no idea what my vocation would be, having little knowledge of the working world. My father knew a signwriter who did some work for Winston Churchill. Being a bit 'arty' this did appeal to me, but I cannot recall why this possibility fell through. Probably not good enough.

Anyway, everything was geared to the war effort and you had to be 'usefully' employed whatever your own inclination may be.

At least we did not have to worry about GCSEs and the like. They had not been invented then. However, it was important to do well in the final term examinations.

Under the tuition of a new young man teacher who was unfit for military service, my ever weak subject of maths – or arithmetic as it was called then, had greatly improved. Figures now made some sense.

As I recall, different papers were set each day, subject by subject, over a week. I was not relishing the prospect, but was not alone as we all set about revision, even down the air-raid shelter.

The first results became available before the end of the week. I was totally 'gobsmacked' to learn that I had top marks in arithmetic. Unbelievable!. My parents were elated, but dad said "I reckon there will have to be a stewards enquiry". Thanks dad!

Geography was always interesting to me, made topical by the various war zones and constant reference to continents and place names.

I was quietly confident about this one, justified by top marks again. Yippee!, who's a clever boy then?

Came mid-week and I got my 'come-uppance'. Only third in English. I should be pleased really, but was getting greedy.

Two to go. History and Science. My results were not exactly 'Whiz kid' stuff, but the overall combined marks were sufficient to edge me into top place. Wake me up, I must be dreaming!

My academic life concluded with a flourish. A few weeks earlier the school captain was admonished for an indiscretion and I was invited to take over. I was not too sure about this. Vice-Captain suited me. Bags of status, but not too much hassle. Ah well, it would not be for too long. Go for it!

Although the main dangers had now passed, several people, such as elderly or alone, remained as regulars down the cellar shelter. This provided a haven of companionship and several stayed almost to the end of the war. These stalwarts became known as the 88 club after our address.

From one such gentleman I obtained a personal introduction to the manager of the huge A.E.C factory at Southall. Famous pre-war as the builders of London buses. In due course I underwent a terrifying interview with this imposing man who oozed authority.

Evidently I passed his scrutiny, being offered a job as a junior stores assistant, starting in a few weeks time.

With many families now receiving the dreaded War Office telegram to inform them that a loved one had been killed in action, or was a prisoner-of-war, it was vitally important that such sad news spread rapidly in order that relatives could be treated with compassion and understanding.

This particularly applied to my parents. They were very mindful of the possibility that in conversation they may ask "How is your husband, heard from him lately?" only to be told, he was killed a couple of weeks ago.

Once again, the famed 'Housewives grapevine' came in useful to alleviate that possibility by word of mouth.

Mum was a shoulder to cry on and on several occasions I witnessed her warm and consoling compassion to distraught lady customers.

Similar principle applied at school, but kids reacted differently. If we knew that someone had lost their dad or brother we would say nothing, but carefully watch their reaction. Maybe they would be very quiet and find a corner of the playground to be alone. That being so, we would leave them for a couple of days, then it would be "Hey Johnny, want a game, come on mate" Hopefully that would break the spell.

Another may act perfectly normally. Presumably with the philosophy that by ignoring such unthinkable news, it would not be true. This was always difficult, leaving one with the uncomfortable feeling 'Surely he must know?' and not being sure of what to do or say.

Fortunately I can only recall a few instances of our school pupils losing relatives.

A newsagents and general store stood on the corner opposite the school, known generally as the 'Tuck shop'.

One lunchtime we were returning from our crossing patrol duties when the lady owner stumbled out with blood on her face.

"He robbed me – went in the junior playground" she yelled.

My colleague and I dropped our boards and dashed into the playground just in time to see a figure climbing the bottom wall which led into the grounds of a convent.

As 13 year olds I am not sure what we would have done had we actually caught up with this character, but the chase prospect was exciting.

Over the wall we went – "There he is" we exclaimed, as a running figure emerged from the trees about 200 yards ahead, but now within sight of the convent main gates.

I was still limping a bit, but we were slowly gaining ground with every stride.

That is, until we reached the convent forecourt. As he dashed through the gates we were confronted by a posse of nuns with outstretched arms. They were definitely not a silent order. The Mother Superior bellowed an order for us to stop. They thought that we were the intruders!

Reluctant to invoke the wrath of God we skidded to a halt. Gasping for breath we tried to splutter an explanation. By the time that we had sorted things out 'Matey' was well away among the streets.

Very disappointed at the outcome we wandered back to school and climbed back over the wall. I dropped straight down into the arms of a waiting copper. "Gotcha – you're nicked!"

As I gabbled a protest my so-called mate stayed hidden on the other side of the wall.

Fortunately, my father had been alerted by all the activity and was able to rescue me before things got out of hand.

Some half-hour late back to class, I crept in very quietly.

My teacher gazed intently and said "Now this had better be good".

"Well Bartlett, get on with it". "Please sir, I have been chasing a robber, got nabbed by some nuns and was then arrested by a copper".

He slowly shook his head, sighed deeply and muttered. "It's good, probably the best I have ever heard. Just where do I go wrong".

In April 1944 we had a very welcome visitor. My mother's nephew from New Zealand.

After the first great war of 1914/18 mums sister Alice married a New Zealander and emigrated to a new life as a sheep farmers wife in Auckland. It was sad that they were never able to fulfil a mutual ambition to meet up again, due in part to the intervention of the war.

In Italy, savage and prolonged fighting had taken place to secure the high ground of Monte Casino, upon which stood the Abbey. 'Kiwi' troops, having fought their way from the Western Desert up through Italy, played a very prominent part in the eventual success. Their resolute bravery and determination was rewarded by an option of 14 days rest and relaxation in England.

My mother was overjoyed at this totally unexpected opportunity to meet Edward 'Teddy', who stayed with us for his leave period.

I was proud to go out with him, resplendent in his new issue uniform with a curled up brim bush hat – Aussie style.

It was amusing when young lads accosted him with the phrase usually reserved for the 'Yanks' 'Got any gum chum?'

He did not smoke so dad was well pleased to see all the packets tumbling out of his kitbag. Every soldier had an allocation of 'Smokes', these were mainly American brands such as the popular Lucky Strike.

Now, what a surprise! I remember sneaking a packet and nearly choking myself as I puffed away hidden down the garden shed.

Overnight of June 6th 1944 we were awakened by the heavy throb of aero engines as massed formations passed nearby. In total contrast to the dark days of 1940/1, this was exciting. They were going the other way!

All the current speculative chat concerned the expected Allied invasion of Europe. There could now be little doubt that this would take place soon. Could this be it?

It was not unusual to see in the distance, formations of bombers heading East on their way to Germany, but this was usually in daylight and certainly not the continual stream that now assailed our ears. This had to be something really big.

We spent a wakeful night. Everyone in the house was up and about early next morning. We all agreed, it's got to be the invasion as we listened intently to the wireless for any first news of this momentous day.

Breakfast was interrupted by another incoming roar. Dashing outside we gazed in awe, as away to the South the sky was filled with aircraft. Although some distance away we could discern that these were Dakota's towing gliders. Contrary to the usual drab appearance, we could make out that every aircraft was distinguished by three broad white bands around the fuselage and wings. This could only be for easy identification and must surely confirm our conclusions.

We had all heard fearsome stories about Hitlers much vaunted 'Atlantic Wall', a seemingly impregnable barrier of defences all along the Channel coastline. Rumours had been rife. Usually any variation of the theme 'Only single men will be in the first wave' – Only those under 25' , or, 'Those with no families'. Whatever the truth, it was fully realised that the inevitable invasion would cost the lives of many fine young men. It had already occurred to me that if the war dragged on for another 3 years, then I too, would be called-up to the forces.

About nine o'clock came the official announcement on the wireless. That in the early hours of June 6th – 'D Day' as it became known. Allied forces had landed on the mainland of Europe. A fairly brief statement that said little, but said it all.

An air of optimistic excitement prevailed throughout the day. Could this really be the beginning of the end?

Little did I imagine then, that 54 years later I would stand on those very beaches. We undertook a battlefield tour of Normandy, visiting the places that have become part of history. The British landing beaches, code named Gold and Sword. Omaha, where the Americans suffered such terrible lossses and Juno, the Canadian area. We also visited the site of the classic British glider borne assault on the vital bridges over the river Orne and adjacent canals at Benouville.

Reverting back to 1944, seven days after 'D Day' the news was good. After a shaky start the bridgehead seemed to be secure and had extended over a 42 mile front.

I was out with my friend Ken after school when the Air-raid sirens sounded. "What's that all about – must be a mistake", surely Jerry was far too busy to make some random attack on London. 'Ignore it, it will go away'. It did, the All-clear sounded.

"Told you so, some silly bugger pressed the wrong button".

A few minutes later we were not so sure, the alert sounded again. What is going on?

So it continued for the rest of that day. Alternating warnings and the all-clear. No 'planes, no gunfire. No nothing.
This was getting silly. Rumours were rife. Some people reckoned that they had heard explosions in the distance. Others had heard that 'Jerry' was sending over silent planes.
A more plausible theory was that they were shelling London with a huge long range gun on the French coast, but if that was so, how did they know when to sound the sirens?
Nothing made sense and it became increasingly obvious that there was some form of a news black-out. This only added to the wild speculation.

The pattern continued the following day. We were up and down the school shelters like 'Yo-Yo's'. After school I met up with Ken about a mile from home. The sirens sounded yet again but we ignored them.
Suddenly, our activities were interrupted by a strange deep throated pulsating drone that increased in volume until a small aircraft hurtled into view travelling very fast and low.

"What the hell is that!" we both exclaimed. "The tails on fire", Questions tumbled, "What's that pipe thing on top?"

It hurtled over and disappeared from view as we stood totally bewildered, listening to the receding sound like a heavily laden motor bike chugging uphill. "It's stopped!", what now?

Seconds elapsed, then 'Whooph' came the sound of a distant explosion.

We had just witnessed the first of many V1 Flying Bombs to reach the Western suburbs. The true situation remained shrouded in mystery as the authorities attempted to cover-up the frightening potential of these secret weapons.

Updated rumours now came thick and fast. They are pilotless planes was the popular opinion. Not so far from the truth really. Suicide pilots was another version. For the moment, they were dubbed 'P Planes'.

As more and more came over the sirens were sounding constantly. On one day there were 17 separate warnings, which caused total confusion.

Our cellar shelter regained all the old regulars. Just as we were thinking it was all over, it was back to square one.

The authorities could no longer disguise or hide the facts. These things were now coming over in some profusion. Within a few days 'Buzz Bombs' became an official fact, instead of exploding gas mains and other imaginative excuses. In fact, the seriousness of the situation prompted another evacuation of children from London.

'Doodlebugs' as they were finally named, were relatively small. 25 feet long, with a wingspan of 17½ feet. They could travel at a speed of over 400mph carrying a warhead of 1870lb. This deadly device had a range of 130 miles.

They normally flew at an altitude of 3000-4000 feet which made it very difficult for the defences, being too low for heavy guns and too high for the light ack-ack.

Launched up a railed concrete ramp, they carried 150 gallons of fuel, sufficient to reach London. When this fuel expired, down they came.

Those which reached the Western suburbs were probably launched from nearer sites around Calais, or maybe given an extra spoonful of fuel for luck.

Post-war records confirm that 11 Flying bombs fell on Ealing, which was then a smaller borough. Subsequently, Southall and Acton were incorporated into the boundery, upon which a further 14 landed causing considerable damage and casualties.

In July, as the onslought reached a height, a 'Doodlebug' struck the large John Sanders departmental store in Ealing Broadway. Fortunately, this was in the early hours and despite considerable widespread damage, casualties were light.

I was now coming to the end of my schooldays and can vividly recall that my final day was spent almost entirely down the playground shelter as these very scary missiles droned pulsatingly over and we all sat with bated breath fearing that sudden engine stop that meant the descent of death and destruction. That dreaded moment came in the afternoon, followed by an earth shaking thud.

A while later a young girl was led away by a compassionate teacher. We all knew the significance.

Later we learned that her home had been hit and her mother killed. What a tragic conclusion to my final day of school life.

My parents bought me a second-hand bicycle for my impending 3 mile journey to work at Southall. This, together with my 14th birthday meant that I could now officially join the A.R.P as a messenger boy. Duties were usually confined to afternoon or early evening, but on one occasion did extend into the night due to a local power failure. Once I started work in a few weeks time the duty hours would have to be revised.

One Sunday morning the Bartlett family were pottering about doing their own things. The sirens had sounded, but life carried on. One advantage of the 'Doodlebugs' was that normally it could be heard approaching, then if the engine stopped there was another 12 seconds to spare before the blast. We had already heard one in the vicinity that morning, but this time the noise was much louder. We stood transfixed, with fingers and everything else crossed as it seemed to pass directly overhead. 'Please keep going' was the fervent albeit selfish plea. We sighed with relief as it droned on before cutting out. Counting down from 12 the 'Crump' of impact seemed quite distant. We dashed upstairs to see the now familiar plume of smoke rising in the direction of Northolt. "Hope Betty is okay" said mum.

Next morning we learned that it had struck the Glaxo Pharmaceutical factory in Greenford. Thankfully it was a Sunday. Any other working day there would have been heavy casualties among the workforce, unless 'Spotters' on the rooftop had identified the immediate danger. Half an hour later another could be heard and again cut-out. This fell in the Brentham area killing 5 people. What a morning! The repeated sirens and all-clear became confusing and certainly worrying that all the explosions had been relatively 'Local'. We had that cold feeling of impending doom, but the rest of the day was fortunately quiet.

A few weeks earlier another one had come down close by. This narrowly missed the Clayponds Isolation Hospital in South Ealing, right on the border with Brentford.

THE EFFECTS OF A FLYING BOMB. UXBRIDGE ROAD WEST EALING JULY 1944

HURRY UP, WE OPEN AT 9am!. CONTINGENT V1 FLYING BOMB DAMAGE TO WEST EALING SHOPPING CENTRE. 1944.

JULY 1944. THE DEVASTATING EFFECT OF A 'V1' FLYING BOMB
WHICH STRUCK JOHN SANDERS DEPARTMENTAL STORE, EALING
BROADWAY IN THE EARLY HOURS. CONSEQUENTLY CASUALTIES
WERE LIGHT.

A PRESENT DAY ILLUSTRATION OF THE LOCATION NOW THE
FACADE OF EALING BROADWAY SHOPPING CENTRE.

It struck in an open space between houses and a day nursery. Damage was widespread, but fortunately casualties were light.

A week later one of the worst incidents in the borough occurred when a Flying Bomb struck the shopping centre in West Ealing. Heavy damage was caused over a wide area and 23 people lost their lives, with many others injured.

They say that lightning does not strike twice, but this area had already suffered badly in 1940 by the effect of a parachute mine when 14 people had been killed.

The day finally arrived for me to start a working life. My head was buzzing with all the input of well intentioned advice. Mother gave me a final 'check over' before I set off on my bike with some trepidation to this milestone in my life.

Shown to my workplace in the stores I relaxed somewhat. Everyone seemed nice and friendly.

It was immediately noticeable that there was a predominence of women, even in the workshop. They were a cheerful bunch, singing and whistling away as they worked the lathes and other machines in a perpetual clatter of noise. Brown overalls and a scrunched up headscarf gave them a uniform appearance.

The men all seemed to be rather elderly, at least to me, but there were several other lads for me to pal up with.

I had an immediate introduction to the air-raid warning drill. Before I had a chance to get to get settled the sirens sounded but nobody moved and just carried on working. 'We wait for the klaxon' said my guide and mentor, then move yourself!

I was shown the location of the air-raid shelter and it was explained that to avoid any loss of production, work carried on after the sirens sounded, relayed through the factory loudspeakers.

Spotters on the roof then determined any immediate danger and would sound a howling klaxon. Basically, this meant run like hell!

In September 1940 the factory had been a specific target for the Luftwaffe. One bomb scored a 'Bullseye' , striking dead centre of the Service Station roof. The interior was badly damaged but fortunately without any casualties as the workforce were safe in shelters away from the building.

Old hands recounted stories about the strange effect of the blast. Seemingly untouched major components such as engines and gearboxes were found to have internal parts shattered. The large bronze gear wheels in differential units seemed to be particularly vunerable and many were found with the gear teeth sheered off, whilst the outer casing had no evident damage.

This meant that every single unit in the place had to be dismantled and examined before production could be resumed.

After a settling in period I was asked whether I would like to try my hand at driving the small electric powered inter-departmental delivery truck. It was all of three seconds before I replied "Er, yes please".

The service station was apart from the vast main factory, then manufacturing Matador field gun tractors and other diverse specialist equipment such as chain flails. These were fitted to the front of tanks and revolved to batter the ground ahead as a form of instant land mine clearance.

I would be handed a list of goods to book out from the stores, load the truck and then deliver all around the sprawling factory. Return loads would be picked up on the way round.

The vehicle had a metal platform at the front on which the driver stood, with one foot on a 'Dead mans pedal'. Once released, the truck juddered to a halt. Steering was by a lever arrangement. Up – left. Down – right. Never having driven anything before this was no problem to me and before long, people were saying 'He can get that thing through the eye of a needle!'

It only carried 5 hundredweight at 6 mph, so there was no chance of doing 'Wheelies'.

Carrying passengers was strictly forbidden, but I soon learned that the attractive young post girls on their rounds were far more interesting goods to carry as they cadged a lift and dangled their legs over the side.

Having led such a sheltered life – in more ways than one – I was naively astounded by some of the antics which took place on the factory floors. One of the components was called a 'U' Bolt. This was a double pronged steel bolt up to eighteen inches long. If one prong was whacked on the floor it set up a vibration. It was a favourite trick of the men to catch any unwary woman bending down or whatever.

If anything, the women were worse than the men for such horseplay. They also had a wicked sense of reprisal.

They would 'gang up' on any persistant male offender. It is perhaps better that details are left to the imagination, but suffice to say that they lost their trousers and thick black grease featured prominently!

They rarely re-offended!

Initially, I was very embarrassed by such goings on and kept out of the way, but soon got used to the squeals, screams and subsequent gales of laughter. I never heard of any complaints, sexual harassment in the workplace had not been invented in those days. It was work hard, play hard.

Working hours were long. For the day shift it was 7.30am through to 6.00pm, with a half day on Saturdays.

As we clocked off in the evening, the night shift would be arriving to maintain non-stop production.

Despite the occasional antics, discipline was strict. I recall being in total awe of the shop foreman who was addressed as sir, as indeed was anyone in a suit.

There was perhaps half a mile of open road between the service station and the expanse of the main factory.

On several occasions I was caught out in the 'no-mans land' when the strident klaxons blared out to signify immediate danger.

There I was, plodding along flat out at 6mph in full view of an approaching 'Doodlebug' with nothing but a field on either side of the road. In future, I must remember to carry a spare pair of trousers!

On one such occasion I was very brave. I had picked up the young post girl and was trundling along, one eye on her and the other on the sky, when we saw one approaching. It was still some miles away when the engine cut out, but these things could occasionally glide a short way before dipping down.

We both hit the deck and I flung myself on top of this young lady and remained there for the next half hour!

How chivalrous can one get?

At lunchtime the young lads used to kick around in the yard with a ball made up of tightly bound rags. Despite the sirens having sounded we were enjoying ourselves, whilst other workers sat around in the sunshine with their sandwiches and tea flasks. Keen ears caught the first sound of that now familiar pulsating throb of a jet propulsion engine. We had a long clear view Eastwards and could now see this horrible thing heading our way.

We all scattered to the vicinity of the air raid shelter, but paused to watch it's progress as it passed over, somewhat lower than usual.

Everyone relaxed, but watched with interest. Having travelled this far, it must soon run out of fuel.

Suddenly, there was a chorus of collective exclamations, loosely interpreted as "The bleedin' things coming back!"

It was now heading back towards us. Dont panic!. Why not, it seemed a good idea to me!

Obviously the guidance mechanism had developed a late fault.

We all scrambled back to the shelter, both scared and fascinated as it passed over again, heading back to London.

"Phew, that's weird, never seen anything like that before". Why pick on us?

It then all happened so quickly. Just as we could see the fiery jet flame at the rear end, this spluttered. The engine coughed and down it plunged. Our view of the explosion was obscured by buildings, but the customary plume of smoke indicated that it must be in the vicinity of some houses.

Immediately, one of our workmates went racing out of the gate yelling something about "She's at home – She's off work sick today". Alas, his worse fears were realised as we heard later that his wife's body had been pulled from the debris.

What an absolute tragedy. We were all stunned. It was a very quiet and subdued workshop that afternoon. Not even the the half-hour 'Music While You Work' over the loud-speakers could lift the gloom. These were music sessions broadcast by the B.B.C mid-morning and afternoon as an aid to production. Sing along or swing bands were the favourites. On the odd occasion that say, a string quartet was introduced, this would be soundly booed, however accomplished they may have been.

For some reason best known to 'Jerry', the period around breakfast time seemed to be favourite to launch V1s. On several occasions as I cycled to work around 7.30am my bike and I parted company. As the throbbing roar came closer one had an instinctive incentive to pedal faster, but 400mph was asking a bit much!

If the engine stopped, then bike one way, you the other. Twelve seconds to find the nearest wall, face down, hands over the head. Every muscle tensed in fearful apprehension. Is this it?.

One morning I rolled to the base of the wall surrounding the St Bernards Mental Hospital. Ugh – too late! What had obviously been a large well fed dog had been there before me. What a mess. With no other clothes to change into I suffered ribald comments all day. My best friends did tell me, many times!

Virtually in the same location a few days later, I approached a scene of activity with police manning barriers across the road.

Approaching with some apprehension, all I could see in the distance was wall rubble across the pavement.

A copper approached. "What's going on" I asked. "It's OK mate, if you are A.E.C you can go past" – "Past what?.

"Oh, it's only a dud Flying Bomb, hit the wall. Been made safe now and they are moving it. You can go to work".

I was not convinced. "You sure about that?"

My bike achieved a new dimension of speed as I hurtled through, but still able to catch a glimpse of the battered but virtually complete missile being hoisted onto a lorry trailer.

This very rare intact secret weapon would provide invaluable data and information. The authorities moved with great speed to cover up the evidence and the wall was rebuilt within days. All very 'Hush hush'. Officially it never happened and I doubt that this incident was ever recorded. Even now, after all these years one can discern the lighter shade of brickwork repairs.

It is worth recording the massive contribution made by the A.E.C factory to the war effort. Some 5000 additional workers were taken on, the majority women. Many thousands of Armoured Cars mounted with a 6 pounder gun were built, together with 8.600 Matador gun towing lorries.

In addition, 3250 Diesel engines for fitment to Matilda tanks and Battle Headquarters vehicles.

Other specialist components were designed and manufactured. Many were secret at the time but ultimately used during the 'D. Day' invasion of Europe.

As the weeks went by we could sense that fewer 'Doodlebugs' were coming over. This was due to a combination of factors. It is now known that along the coastline known as 'Doodlebug Alley', a mass of medium anti-aircraft guns had been assembled.

Firstly, fighter aircraft would attempt an intercept out over the English Channel. The latest Typhoon and Tempest fighters were aircraft capable of matching the speed of the V1. However, it was hazardous to shoot them down from close range as the warhead could explode. Pilots were not too keen on that prospect.

Some enterprising aces flew alongside and tipped the wings with their own, causing the missile to plunge into the sea. If these methods failed the V1 flew on straight and true into a steel curtain of gunfire through which it had to pass. The success rate improved every day and many were now being blown up in the air.

Added to this, the invasion of Normandy was gathering pace as a break-out was achieved over a wide front and some of the launch sites were over-run by Allied forces. Other launch sites were identified and plastered by bombers.

The Germans did however, have another trick up their sleeve as about 1000 Flying Bombs were slung under aircraft and launched in mid-air.

By the time that Paris was liberated on August 25th, the 'Doodlebug' menace was virtually over.

Post war statistics indicate that a total of 9251 were launched against Southern England in a relatively short period. Of these, a creditable 4621 were destroyed before reaching their target. The 4630 that did get through caused considerable damage and killed some 6000 people, with another 16.000 injured.

The now recognised Borough of Ealing suffered quite severely during this onslought.

Eleven struck the then Ealing area. 7 fell in Acton and a further 7 in Southall. A total of 91 persons were killed, 204 seriously injured and 694 injured to a lesser degree.

181 residential homes were destroyed by Flying Bombs alone.

Yet again we were lulled into a false sense of security. Surely now it must be all over? Hitler could not have any more surprises – could he?

On September 8th, just about tea time, we heard a deep rumbling explosion in the distance. No sirens had sounded. Not to worry, it could be anything.

The next morning our shop customers were all talking about a big explosion in Chiswick. It was the same at work, something about a gas main going up.

Later that day a wireless news bulletin briefly mentioned that a gas main had exploded in a Western suburb causing some casualties.

It does seem out of character, but for some reason my parents and sister wanted to go and have a look. In the evening we took a bus to Chiswick and made our way to Staveley Road. We had all seen enough destruction to last a lifetime, but I can now understand that the motivation was not to 'Gawp', but a strong feeling that something was going on, although no-one could figure out what this may be.

We were confronted by a terrible scene. Many houses had been flattened and others damaged by blast. One could only conclude 'that was some ruddy gas main!'

People were very uneasy. There was the general feeling that despite the official assurances we were being 'conned' again, similar to the Flying Bomb episode.

Every possible explanation was discussed in detail but rockets certainly did not feature. Our knowledge of such things did not extend beyond Guy Fawkes night.

By sheer coincidence of course, more 'gas mains' blew up around London over the coming days. In fact, it was not until November 10th that Churchill announced to Parliament and thereby the nation that the recent 'incidents' had been caused by a very advanced ballistic missile equipped with a one ton warhead. The deadly V2, forerunner of mans conquest of space. During that interim period approximately 100 missiles had fallen on London, giving the gas board a very bad name!

Fuelled by alcohol and liquid oxygen they were launched from Holland to arrive in London just 4 minutes later, descending at a speed of 2.400mph they created a supersonic boom. This was something that we had never heard of and would not understand anyway.

Looking out of our top window one early morning my father insisted that he had seen a bright comet-like tail ascending into the far distant dawn sky. We were very sceptical when he said 'Bet it's a rocket'.

'Nah, it can't be' we exclaimed. Until a few minutes later came the deep rumbling sound of an explosion somewhere in the capital. It does seem incredulous that he could have seen the ascent from such a distance, but equally a remarkable co-incidence that fully justified his response "Told you so".

The V2s were devastating on impact. One hit the Deptford branch of Woolworths store crowded with shoppers killing 160, mainly women and children.

There was just no answer to this menace. Launch sites were small and easily constructed. Any area of hard concrete would suffice. No defence or early warning – except dad! – could be devised. The population had to adopt a fatalistic attitude and carry on a normal life with the oft quoted 'If it's got your name on it'.

The lunch time hooter sounded at the factory and we all piled out eager for our kick-about. Someone had even dug out a real leather football from the depths of a garden shed. Suddenly a huge explosion stopped us in our tracks, followed by a second 'Boom'. Incomprehensible then, but the sonic bang as the rocket re-entered the earths atmosphere. A huge pall of smoke began to rise about a mile away towards Brentford. "Come on lad's, lets go" came the cry as we grabbed our bikes and set off as fast as we could pedal to see if we could provide any assistance.

The Great West Road was, and still is, lined with factories. The missile had struck the Packard Car Company near to the well known Gillette Corner at Brentford.

"Oh my God" we all exclaimed, viewing a scene of carnage. There was little that we could do to help. The area was already swarming with American servicemen from the nearby base. They must have responded very quickly, followed by the emergency services. We could hardly bear to watch as bodies were being excavated and laid out side by side along the pavement. Mum's and dad's who would not be returning home to their families that evening.

The air was polluted with that pungent sulphuric dust pervading the throat, nose and eyes. Thankfully providing an excuse for the tears that trickled down my cheeks.

The line of bodies lengthened as the injured were taken away to an American field hospital that had been hastily set up. Those G.Is were doing a great job.

We left that scene with heavy hearts to wend our way back to work. I never did hear the casualty figures. Such details did tend to be suppressed, although it usually become known locally in due course.

Fortunately, during that period Ealing was spared the impact of a V2 Rocket, but it is now known that possibly the only missile to malfunction, did so over Ealing in November.

Over all the intervening years this has provided the only logical explanation of an incident that had puzzled everyone at the time and still remembered even now.

I have met several people of late, all have been just a few years younger than me and still at school at the time.

Several recall being at assembly. This would place the time at something like 9.15am.

A massive explosion rent the air, but this was something different. It seemed to come from overhead and created an atmospheric pressure that bore down on head and shoulders like a heavy blanket.

One chap remembered that his assembly lost composure until the head-master said something like "Steady lads, we are all safe. Now let us pray for those less fortunate".

A lady described to me that at the local girls school there was some panic as girls screamed and ran from the hall assembly.

I had just started work at the A.E.C factory in Southall and can well recall the strange rumbling shock wave that spread across the sky like ripples on a pond as everyone exclaimed "What the bloody hell was that!"

It became a topic of conversation among the workforce but without any subsequent explanation or evidence of a 'strike' anywhere.

My parents described similar sensations as the stock trembled and fell off the shelves as the thunder like rumble spread across the Autumn sky.

Days of speculation followed – 'What was it – Where did it fall?'. No evidence emerged and gradually the incident faded into obscurity until 60 years later we have a probable explanation.

Archive records reveal that pieces of the rocket casing were scattered over a wide area of South Ealing. Larger engine like components were located to the North of Ealing Broadway.
These were subsequently identified as V2 Rocket components by the authorities, but we of course, remained entirely ignorant of their findings.

It seems logical now to conclude that entering the earths atmosphere at 2.400 mph would have created a sonic boom to co-incide with the explosion, thus intensifying the detonation shock waves.

Of course, we are still left with the unanswerable question. Where would it have landed had the hand of fate not intervened? Perhaps it is better not to dwell on that.

This new technology of rocketry was fascinating. A group of us youngsters at work decided to experiment by constructing a small missile with a metal tube, a cone shaped nose piece and a small outlet at the other end. Propellant? – How about red match heads?. We laboriously chipped off sufficient to fill the tube and gently compacted them down.
The only highly technical form of ignition that we could think of was a candle!
One day we gave the customary kick-about a miss. We were ready for lift-off. Theoretically, constant heat from the candle would

eventually ignite the match heads. It was then a matter of 'Whoosh' – or more likely splutter, fizzle and fall over. We found a quiet corner of the workshops, deserted during lunchtime. A rather 'Heath Robinson' launch pad had been constructed to hold our 'Rocket' at a steep angle.

The candle was lit and we waited at a safe distance – and waited – and waited. Twenty minutes passed. Nothing happened. Interest was waning. 'Told you it wouldn't work'.

Suddenly, in a shower of sparks 'WHOOSH'. We were all stunned as this thing took off faster than our eye could follow, leaving just a white smoke trail as it burst clean through the asbestos sheeted roof sending fragments tumbling down.

'Oh my gawd!' , let's get out of here! Fortunately we were close to the rear exit to the air raid shelters, so grabbing the hot launch pad contraption we scuttled out to the rear of the workshops. Once out of sight we split up to stroll nonchalently round to the front of the building with looks of benign innocence to enquire "What's going on?"

By now, various types of boss men were accumulating to ponder the cause of the damage which had brought people running to investigate. Inside the air was filled with sulphur fumes from the burnt match heads.

We all kept quiet and no conclusions were ever reached. On reflection, a grossly irresponsible escapade, but we were only 14 year olds and certainly did not expect such a spectacular result. We always wondered where our 'Rocket' finished up. Maybe it is still in orbit among the space debris of later years!

The last V2 Rocket of 1054 fell at Orpington in Kent on March 27th 1945.

Despite all the terror and havoc that they wrought, neither 'V' weapon proved capable of altering the inevitable course of the war. By the time that they became operational the end was already in sight. Had they been developed even a few months earlier the consequences do not bear thinking about. Particularly had they been aimed at the English Channel ports crammed to bursting with the 'D. Day' invasion fleets and hundreds of thousand men.

Throughout the spring Allied forces advanced across Europe to enter Germany, whilst Russian forces pushed ever forward from the East. An air of optimism prevailed. Surely now, it can only be a matter of time before it is finally all over.

People had a smile on their faces and a spring in their step. Life on the home front was assuming an air of normality within the confines of continuing severe rationing and other restrictions. One very encouraging feature was that on April 25th the black-out regulations were relaxed, but after 5 years of total darkness people were too conditioned to take full advantage. The only disappointed characters were the Air-raid Wardens. No longer would they be able to yell 'Put that ruddy light out!'

News came that the Russians had reached Berlin and among a profusion of rumours, one that Hitler had committed suicide in his bunker. Dare we hope that the end was nigh?

The wireless stayed on all day to pick up every scrap of news, duly passed on with great enthusiasm.

This is it – the greatest day! Germany has surrendered. Tomorrow May 8th 1945 has been declared 'VE Day' – Victory Europe. It really is all over.

What a fantastic feeling. Everyone is singing and dancing in the streets. Joy and relief is mirrored in every face as complete strangers embrace and kiss in a rare breakdown of British reserve. Street parties are being organised and massed crowds are already converging on Buckingham Palace where the King and Queen are due to appear on the balcony with 'Winnie' as Churchill was known. Tomorrow could be quite a day!

I joined my parents in a happy 'Wrecking spree', ripping down the remaining black-out and prising off the wooden shutters. Off came all the window sticky tape and 5 long years of gloom were dispelled as sunlight streamed in to enhance our carefree mood.

Anticipating the day, mum had made up new curtains which had to go up today! Dad's mumbled 'I'll do it tomorrow' was swiftly squashed! That task completed, I helped dad to drape 3 huge flags over the parapet nailed to long poles. The union flag fluttered proudly between the 'Stars & Stripes' and the Russian red flag. They joined thousands of others appearing as if by magic in every street to provide a riot of colourful patriotism.

With a lifetimes experience crammed into my childhood, I had matured from a naive little kid into a prematurely matured young man of 15. There can be no more fitting conclusion than to quote the words of Winston Churchill when Britain stood alone against the German might 5½ weary years earlier. "I have nothing to offer but blood, sweat and tears. If we should fail, the whole world will sink into the abyss of a new dark age".

The British people did not fail. On reflection, I feel very priviledged to have lived through that extraordinary period of history and proud of the contribution made by our 'ordinary' family.

My parents epitomised the unified spirit, determination and self sacrifice that prevailed on the 'Home front', where every man, woman and child 'did their bit' to the best of their ability and opportunity.

Our shop opened as usual as we scuttled around doing all the jobs that mum had lined up. Although a national holiday had been declared, dad reckoned that we should keep faith with our customers, but he did compromise with a noon closure.

A few customers justified his thoughts, but in the main these were shelter regulars calling in to retrieve all their bits and pieces from the cellar, such as bed linen, mats and photo's etc.

It was evident that the overiding desire now was to remove all reminders of that existence as quickly as possible, literally within hours of the cessation of hostilities.

Within a couple of days the cellar shelter had been stripped bare of all traces of 5 years occupation, leaving the double bunks standing rather forlorn.

With none of the mats on the cold stone floor or curtains that covered the bunks, the cellar sounded hollow as we stood around contemplating the sudden dramatic change. "Well" said dad "This place certainly came in handy over the years. We are going to miss all the familiar faces. Rather like having a big family down here"

Typically mum had the last word "This place could do with a good sweep up now". At which dad remembered an urgent appointment elsewhere!

Living on a main road we missed out on a street party but my parents were invited to all those in the neighbouring side streets.

In mid-morning all the church bells started pealing. Such a joyous albeit discordant sound as each vied to produce the loudest and melodious 'concert'.

Being a 14 year old lad but out at work I was something of a 'Tweenie' which proved to be a great advantage.

I was able to wander from party to party in the afternoon looking suitably lost and appealing. This guaranteed that I could hover around the kids parties and be offered cakes, sandwiches and other 'goodies' by those women who had scrimped and saved from the still meagre rations to provide such treats for the children.

As dusk fell I suddenly grew up to be a worker and thus joined the adult parties with the prospect of beer and kisses.

All the tea tables were cleared away, wind up gramophones or piano's dragged out into the street and the bonfires stoked up with torn down black-out shutters and blinds. Some of them became huge and looked positively dangerous.

As darkness fell these were lit to cheers and the parties began in earnest. I recall putting potatoes in one fire, but they came out like lumps of solid charcoal!

One of the biggest thrills was when the street lamps came on again after a lapse of almost 6 years. Everyone cheered and could not believe the illumination, having been so used to the intense darkness of the black-out. Surprisingly, most of the bulbs still worked – or had the authorities anticipated the day and had people quietly creeping round replacing them?

We then noticed that searchlights were illuminating the sky over London. I nipped back home to have a look from the top window. Two powerful lights converged to form a steady 'V' as others danced around the skyline reminiscent of the scene during the 'Blitz'.

Red glows were also becoming visible as the victory bonfires took hold.

Perhaps it is just as well that I cannot clearly recall the details of that night. It all seems to be a haze of singing and dancing. Maybe I did sneak a few beers!

We all went to bed that night tired, but relaxed and happy as the strains of music and the tang of smoke still drifted in the night air. It had been a wonderful day. We slept well, for tomorrow is the dawn of a new era.

And so, after almost 6 years of conflict, what happened to the Bartlett 'gang' in the years ahead?

My father remained as school caretaker for another 6 months until his predecessor returned from service in the Royal Navy.
Resuming life as a shopkeeper, devoid of all the wartime diversions and activities proved rather mundane. He was a fidget, always under mum's feet. It was no surprise when he 'dabbled' in painting and decorating again at my mothers suggestion. She was quite happy to manage the shop.
In the meantime, council workmen moved in to dismantle all the cellar strengthening and restore the area to its original function as

a storage facility. At the same time, the premises were given a 'face lift' to finally eradicate the bomb damage.

My parents retired in 1956. Unfortunately, dad did not live to enjoy a long well earned rest, passing away in 1961 at the age of 71. Mother kept as 'Bright as a button' until we sadly said goodbye in 1976 at the age of 85.

Being that much older and stationed in England, brother Ted was demobilised quite quickly to resume a happy family life with Betty. He re-joined the 'Big house' as head of staff until the death of his lady employer. Shamefully, this lovely house was demolished shortly afterwards and yet another block of flats now occupies the site.

Ted's remaining years to retirement were spent as a gardener, but he continued to produce beautiful furniture and marquetry work as a hobby. He died of a heart condition in 1979 at the age of just 66, leaving his wife and one son.

Brother Bern certainly drew the 'short straw'. Just prior to the end of the war in Europe, he was shipped out from West Africa to the far East where the war continued against Japan. Firstly to India, then on to Burma. Thankfully, by the time that he reached the areas of conflict, Japan had surrendered following the atomic bombs on the cities of Horoshima and Nagasaki.

It was not until late 1946 that he eventually arrived home to catch up on a very belated honeymoon. "Er, sorry about that Joyce, I'm only 5 years late!"

Like so many other returning servicemen he found it difficult to settle down to civilian life and after a spell as chief mechanic for a local coach company, with Joyce they opened a camping equipment shop. The business thrived as people looked to pursue cheap leisure activities again. They had three children, a daughter and two sons, one of whom manages the now diversified company specialising in winter sports equipment.

Having retired to Dorset, this devoted couple were together for over 60 years until Bern passed away in 1996 aged 79.

As I pen this conclusion, Joyce is still enjoying life as a sprightly young lady of 85.

Sister Ivy took up accountancy for a clothing chain store. Brother-in-law Arthur left the Auxiliary Fire Service to work at a local bus depot. They had one son who ultimately entered a full time career with the Royal Air Force as a helicoptor winch-man. Ivy died of leukemia in 1987 aged 78.

Arthur died of cancer aged 69 in 1964.

My evacuation foster dad Bill died prematurely at the age of 60, but 'auntie' Connie reached the ripe old age of 94 before passing away in 2005.

We kept in touch with this lovely lady for nigh on 65 years and visited as often as possible. Her recall of my brief stay was quite remarkable. To friends and neighbours I was always referred to as her 'little vaccy'.

Whenever we visited she would jokingly offer us corned beef and pineapple chunks for our meal, after which I would still have to ask 'Please may I leave the table?'

So, what happened to me?. Now that could be a long and separate story. Kicking about with that tied up bundle of rags during lunch breaks at the A.E.C factory certainly had a lot to answer for, but determined that I would live a very full and rewarding life.

Within weeks of the end of the war in Europe we had formed a football team – albeit completely useless!

Selection was not difficult. If you had a pair of the old solid toecap 'Clodhopper' boots, then you must be good enough . Kit was contrived from army surplus baggy shorts and socks, topped by ordinary shirts dyed yellow.

We lost the first game 13 – 1, which suggested a change of tactics or all eleven players!

It poured with rain throughout the game and the inferior wartime yellow dye proved to be useless on material but very effective on skin.

As we stripped off in the dressing room this resembled an aviary of canaries!

By now I worked in the stores office, consequently, as the only 'white collar' worker among the lads I was talked into becoming the secretary of this so-called football team.

However, we prospered, and within two years became the first British youth team to re-establish sporting links with the continent by playing 2 games in Belgium. A really great adventure in those days.

A year later in 1948 I had an enforced break with almost 2 years National Service in the R.A.F.

Having related the story of a little boy's war, it seems appropriate to conclude this narrative with a rather light hearted account of the aftermath as a young man.

Mindful that this book will be read by many young people I prefer to leave interpretation of the eloquence of certain R.A.F instructors to the individual reader!

Among my 18th birthday cards the dreaded large buff envelope dropped through the letter box. 'You will report to R.A.F West Kirby, The Wirral, Cheshire'.

Rail vouchers were enclosed, together with a list of do's and dont's.

Two weeks hence I would now become one of many thousand National Service 'Bods' milling about the countryside on their way to Naval, Army, or Air Force camps, wherever the authorities or 'Lucky dip' determined.

THE AUTHOR AS A YOUNG R.A.F NATIONALSERVICEMAN. 1948

THE AUTHOR – THIRD FROM LEFT – UNDERGOING BOMB STORAGE AND DISPOSAL COURSE AS A NATIONAL SERVICEMAN. 1948. THE BOMB FEATURED IS A 4000lb 'COOKIE' AS DROPPED BY THE R.A.F.

Despite living through the war years, in the late forties we were surprisingly naive and the later term 'Virgin Soldiers' was very apt.

On the appointed day my father accompanied me to the station where a motley collection of pasty faced pimply lads from all walks of life were assembling in little groups awaiting the train to Liverpool. My brother Bernard unexpectedly arrived to stuff a couple of pound notes in my pocket – lot of money in those days, and to offer well chosen words of advice.

He had finished the war years as a Warrant Officer and I suspect that he had some idea of what 8 weeks 'Basic Training' or 'Square-bashing' as it was known, really meant!

On the journey we made temporary friendships. We were all in the same boat – or train, so to speak. One lad proved to be a right cheerful soul. He related horror stories passed on by someone, who knew someone who had been at West Kirby.

We laughed nervously and said "Nah, that can't be true. They wouldn't do that – Would they?"

We were soon to learn. They could and did!

Wandering shambolically off the train at Lime Street station we were confronted by an immaculately uniformed R.A.F Flight Sergeant, who pointed his pace stick at any likely candidate and roared "You for West Kirby? – Get over there and stand still you 'orrible little man".

Gradually he gathered together a quivering collection of misfits. Long, short, tall, fat and skinny. A miscellany of British youth. He viewed us with a look of utter distaste and slowly shook his head. Approaching each of us to close range he snarled, "What's your name – 'ave you got one?", then made a tick on his clip-board with obvious relish.

His numbers crunched he handed over to a couple of hovering Corporals whose job it was to shuffle this untidy mob into two wavy lines by commands shouted loudly in what appeared to be a foreign language.

FORMUP IN DOOS – SHUDUP – STANSTILL – QUAAAAAK MCH – AIFT, AIFT, AIFT, OIT, AIFT, to 'March' us through the streets of Liverpool to the suburban line station.

Sympathetic smiles on the faces of bystanders suggested that they had seen it all before. Another week, more little lambs to the slaughter!. A fruit and veg' stall holder sang out with obvious glee "YOU'LL BE SOOOORY".

On arrival at camp we were taken to the bedding store where sheets and blankets etc were unceremoniously dumped onto our outstretched arms whilst trying desperately to cling onto our small suitcases. Woe betide any lad who dropped something. "PICK IT UP YOU DOZY .... IDIOT".

It is fair to say that we were not happy at our welcome. Images of Biggles and reflected glory of wartime exploits were fading fast. Was this really the glamorous R.A.F – the Brylcream boys?

Allocated to a billet an uneasy calm descended as we got to know our new bedside mates and struggled to master the art of bed making. This tranquility was short lived. The door crashed open and in strode a big imposing Flight Sergeant, who, in a broad Irish accent, roared "STAND BY YOUR BEDS – STAND STILL YOU 'ORRIBLE WEEDY LOOKING RABBLE".
"This filthy pig-sty will be your home for the next 8 weeks. IT WILL BE CLEAN. So clean that I will be able to lick food off the floor. WON'T IT? If not, you will ALL lick the floor 'till it shines".
"Now get to it. I will be back at 8 o'clock tonight".
A smart about turn and crash went the door.

We stood dumb with shock and awe. Immediate desertion became a popular option. Some of the lads were close to tears at this sudden culture shock.

We had been issued with 'Eating irons' and a mug and had experienced our first unimaginative meal in the mess. Thoughts of investigating the N.A.A.F.I in the evening had now gone out of the window.

We found the cleaning cupboard and set-to. The first contribution to team building. To our eyes the billet was already spotless, but for 2 solid hours we scrubbed and polished 'till our arms ached and the hut positively gleamed.

Dead on time the door was flung open. A mad scramble ensued to stand by our beds – we had learnt that much already.

The Flight Sergeant entered slowly and deliberately, his eyes darting everywhere as he paced down the room.

The tension was unbearable.

In a split second the mood changed and he became a fireball. Wiping his finger down a metal bed leg he roared 'FILTHY' and turned the poor lads bed and possessions upside down. The top of a locker door was the next target. Gazing at his supposedly dirty finger with a look of disgust he tipped all the contents out to the floor, shouting as he did so ' ----------- DISGRACEFUL". So it went on as he ranted on about hygiene and poncy mummies boys. "Mummy aint here now. You come to me and I'll kiss you better".

"You 'ave one hour to clean this S...house properly." We tensed for the inevitable door crash.

Stunned with shock it went very quiet until one lad said, "Come on fellas, let's get cracking". Our first example of leadership qualities emerging.

On the dot this nice friendly Flight Sergeant returned, strode in and to our utter astonishment snarled "Much better. Now get to bed. You may think you've had a hard day, just wait until tomorrow. Good-night lads".

Applied psychology or what?.

At 06.30 we were blasted out of bed by the strident noise of a bugle relayed through the billet loudspeakers. Dawn Reveille. Oh my God – what would today bring?

There was a scramble to the outside ablution block to grab a cubicle or sink where several lads shaved for the very first time. At least it was summer. Wouldn't fancy this performance in the depths of winter!

We consoled each other. It can't be that bad. Only got 7 weeks 6 days to go now!

Little did I know then, that my initial training would actually extend over 15 weeks!

That first day became a blur of commands at the double. Firstly to be kitted out as airmen. Battle-dress. Horrible stiff and pimply leather boots. Best Blue uniform and thankfully softer boots for 'walking-out'. Back packs, groundsheets and webbing all came flying into our arms until we staggered back to the billet loaded like donkeys to sort this lot out.

Everything was creased like wrinkled prunes and the iron would be in great demand, but at least we may eventually look like airmen.

We were ordered to put the battledress on NOW! and fall in outside in 5 minutes, to spend the rest of the day marching up and down, to halt, about turn and all the other rudiments of drill. What a shambles. Some lads just could not co-ordinate to march properly, others didn't know left from right. The corporals went purple with frustration and even invented new words of profane encouragement!

Oh yes, in between, a visit to Sweeney Todd the demon barber of West Kirby!

A jovial character who obviously derived sadistic pleasure from his occupation. He allowed about 2 minutes for each recruit. Finesse or style did not figure in his mind as he wielded a mini version of a hover lawnmower and swept this over carefully preened heads to reduce them to the appearance of hedgehogs with alopecia. Back at the billet the universal cry was "What's my girl going to say?" or "I'll never pull again".

Came the evening and we were shattered, but the billet had to be cleaned again, uniforms pressed and a start made on our boots. The tip was, to apply polish with the handle of a hot spoon, at the same time, spitting and polishing with a small circular action. At this stage, it seemed like a hopeless task.

In the midst of all this frenetic activity that nice chap the Flight Sergeant burst in and gazed around at 14 petrified little 'erks' as we were called.

"RIGHT – 'OO PLAYS FOOTBALL?"

I thought, there must be a catch. Never volunteer. Everyone told me that.

Silence, no movement. He relished the moment, turned a delicate shade of purple and in a cold menacing tone said "Us sergeants 'ave a big strong very 'ard team. We 'ave a pitch tonight and we're goin' to play someone and goin' to win – AINT WE! he bellowed.

"Er, yes Flight Sergeant" came a thin reply from strangled throats.

"I want one volunteer from this filthy pig sty of an 'ut.

Otherwise you will all be on a charge".

I pondered – Shall I? It might be a good skive and put me in his good books, so I took a pace forward in what I thought to be regulation style.

The roof well nigh lifted off as he roared "STAND STILL – WHO TOLD YOU TO MOVE?"

Then it dawned, I might just be volunteering. He put his face to mine and snarled "Are you a volunteer laddie?".

There seemed to be something wrong with my voice. A high pitched squeak came out. "Yes Flight Sergeant, I'm a goalkeeper".

He was a changed man.

"You are a brave man. I shall recommend you for the V.C. - ----- posthumously! Cos I'm a centre-forward and I kill goalkeepers. Report to the field at 19.00 hours sharp".

In uniform forty eight hours and already a hero, having saved 14 mates single handed!

A motley collection of scared lads faced the Sergeants team. They were all over us and having dived to put two of his headers round the post he was not a pretty sight as he glared hate.

The game was only ten minutes old when he came storming through with the ball at his feet. Ah well, here we go and down I went. Trouble was, he did not do any of the customary niceties like jump, draw back etc. His shooting boot crashed into my knee and I was paralysed with pain.

That night passed in a dream like state as I was taken to the base hospital and after examination was injected to relieve the almost unbearable pain.

After three weeks treatment the specialist said "We are going to send you for convalescence. Do you know a place called Chessington?" "No sir. Heard of the zoo". One thing you do learn is quick thinking. Chessington was only a long bus ride from my home!.

I managed to hang out for 4 weeks in the lap of luxury at the rehabilitation centre. Home every evening and week-ends. Resplendent in a paler 'Hospital Blue' uniform, my bus fares were never taken.

I did feel a fraud with only 48 hours service. The rest of the patients were old hands, some still recovering from war wounds.

A leisurely routine. Up at 8.o'clock to enjoy a tasty breakfast followed by perhaps a ramble in the countryside or light exercises. What a life, this is more like it!

Actually, the knee was fine, but every Thursday evening I slapped it with wet flannels to induce swelling that completely baffled the specialist and gained me another week of comfort.

That is, until he changed his day to Wednesday and declared me fully fit – Get out!.

Another day at home before I returned to West Kirby and fortune smiled again. The entire country was blotted out by one of those dense 'Smogs' that we used to suffer from in those days.

Main line trains were cancelled as transport ground blindly to a halt.

I telephoned the guardhouse to avoid being posted A.W.O.L (Absent without leave).

The fog persisted. At this rate, if I played my cards right, I could be de-mobbed without completing basic training!

No such luck. The fog cleared and I finally reported back to West Kirby to be attached to a new intake of recruits. Back to square one. By now, my original mates were looking forward to their passing-out parade.

I soon realised that my prolonged absence had created a problem. Initially, the new lads were in total awe of someone who had been in for almost 8 weeks and even had a pressed uniform – thanks mum – and boots that had something of a shine on them.

The trouble was, that I had the lowest service number which still comes readily to mind 2404067. This meant appointment as billet leader, class leader etc. Personally, I fancied Squadron Leader but it didn't work like that!

At least I knew what to expect, which gave a head start for hut inspections.

Day after day we marched, drilled and polished until everything merged together in a blur of harsh discipline that gradually formed an awareness of team spirit and pride. There was a saying, If it moves, salute it. If it stays still, paint it white.

Our left shoulders bore bruises from the impact of the old Lee-Enfield .303 rifles as we slammed them down at slope arms. We scraped toilet seats with a razor blade. Cut grass around the hut with scissors and even washed and polished the coal in the billet coal bin.

Our boots were gradually transformed from pimply dull leather into shaving mirrors.. Nearing pass-out day, even the brass eyelets on our boots were polished. Stark raving mad, but then, incredibly acceptable to our new way of life.

By comparison to the namby-pamby attitudes of today, this harsh regime contravened every aspect of human rights, but transformed us into very smart and proud young men with standards that have held us in good stead throughout our lives.

On pass-out parade day we were voluntarily up at 4am to check and re-check our uniforms, helping each other to remove the slightest speck of dust or mark on our webbing belts.

What an intense feeling of pride. Rifle butts were given a final polish and we waddled to the assembly point on our heels to avoid cracking the thick layer of polish that gleamed in the morning sunshine.

We came to attention. The band struck up with the R.A.F march past and with a tingle down our spines we completed the parade as fully fledged airmen. An experience that I will never forget. We really had become the best.

Perhaps the most extraordinary moment came at the end of the parade. Our drill instructor Flight Sergeant and corporals came round to shake our hands and say "Well done lads, bloody marvellous".
To our astonishment, they were actually human beings!

Meanwhile, my trade training posting had come through. I was to be an 'Equipment Assistant', or storekeeper in plain English. Another 6 weeks course at Credenhill near Hereford. A camp that is now the headquarters of the S.A.S.

Again, my low service number 'saddled' me with the duties of whatever leader, but this time with a promotion – Intake leader. This meant that I had to march the entire 'mob' of trainees to and from courses.
Wow, the power! Almost without realising I became a clone of those drill instructors, bawling and shouting orders. I suspect a right basket!

Near the end of the course I was asked whether I would like to 'volunteer' for an explosives qualification. Basically a munitions storekeeper, but to include a specialist bomb disposal and poison gas training programme that would last another 8 weeks.
At this rate, my original theory that I could be de-mobbed without actually doing anything was looking quite feasible!

I was sent to a disused Fleet Air Arm aerodrome on the East coast which had vast expanses of prohibited beaches.

We had a lovely time blowing up all sorts of surplus bombs and ammunition. All very exciting until the day that we were let loose to actually de-fuse a small bomb.

Sent out to a safe distance, it was a lonely walk. We were each talked through the procedure by radio link. My hands were shaking from the cold – That's my excuse.

Anyway, the fuse came out, nothing went bang and I returned to the billet to change my trousers!

By the end of this course I had been in for 7 months. Potentially almost half the normal service time.

Eventually I was posted to a remote bomb dump on the edge of the Yorkshire moors. A lonely outpost with little recreational facilities.

Much of our time was spent in disposing of war surplus explosives. We had some magnificent bonfires out on the moors interposed with a few big bangs.

Over enthusiasm on one occasion brought a call from an airfield some ten miles away 'Has an aircraft crashed in your vicinity?'

We took turns in guarding a 'secret' Mustard Gas storage facility tucked away in the countryside. This meant donning protective suits to wander round and turn on or off large valves which controlled the flow of this liquid through underground pipes. Didn't like that job!

Also unpopular was guard duty at a disused aerodrome at Marsden Moor, scene of the English civil war battle. Stories abounded of the ghost that appeared at the front gate in the attire of a Roundhead soldier, accompanied by a large dog.

One night, the sensible and reliable corporal in charge of our party, heard a noise in the night, went out to investigate and returned a gibbering wreck.

He swore that he had seen this apparition exactly where and how the stories related. This incident was taken seriously and recorded by the station commander to join earlier reports. Where was I? Under the bed covers!

My theories about length of service seemed to filter through to the authorities. Earlier recruits were de-mobbed after 18 months. Later intakes did 20 months, but in my case, almost 2 years. Every enquiry was brushed aside, 'It's in hand'.

After 23 months they let me go. I reckon that they got their own back for all those weeks I went 'Walkabout'.

Duty done, I returned to resume work at the A.E.C factory. Meanwhile, the football club had prospered. My father – 'Pop' as he was popularly known, had done a great job of holding the reins whilst I had been away.

My future wife had joined the football team youth club and promptly diverted my hitherto total interest in football.

We were eventually married on Boxing Day – appropriate or what! in 1954 and had son Gordon a year later.

In those days we must have been totally mad. in 1965 after 2 years of frustrating paperwork we finally overcame a bureaucratic nightmare to organise a momentous 4000 mile overland coach tour to the Soviet Union at the height of the so-called 'Cold War' when East/West relations were on a knife edge.

However, this defied all the pessimists and despite dire warnings proved to be a truly remarkable goodwill success.

By doing so, we became only the second amateur team to undertake such a venture, the first being a university team way back in the early thirties.

In 1968, another even more ambitious overland tour to the Balkans ended abruptly in Czechoslovakia when we became caught up in the Soviet led 'Warsaw Pact' invasion of that country. Our subsequent adventures and escape into Austria is a story in itself. Ultimately we established a record of 92 matches against foreign opposition in travels throughout 14 countries of Europe.

Now, 60 years after that humble 'Rag ball' beginning, I am proud to be president of Viking Sports Football Club with its remarkable record of initiative and achievement.

Leaving the A.E.C in 1967 I was then employed by an American fork-lift truck company as a Service Administration Manager.

With a total change of vocation I then became a social worker with children in care until early retirement in 1996.

Throughout the years, my involvement in many varied community projects has afforded me great pleasure and satisfaction. In 2001 I was humbly priviledged to be placed on the New Years Day Parade 'London Roll of Honour' for service to the community of the London Borough of Ealing.

Beryl and I still live in West Ealing. Happily together for 50 years now, we have been blessed with a fine son and daughter-in-law who have made us proud of their own achievements in life, above all, two lovely grandchildren, Amanda and Craig.

THOUGH WE MAY NOT FORGET THOSE DISTANT YEARS

A SHADOW PLAY OF EMOTIVE FEARS

YOU WERE AS YET UNBORN, A LIFE TO COME

NOW PAUSE A WHILE AND TURN YOUR MIND

TO FOREBEARS, THOSE ANCESTRAL KIND

WHO BRUSHED THE WINGS OF DEATH IN DAILY TOIL

THAT YOU MAY TREAD THIS FREEDOM SOIL.

RB.

A FINAL PAUSE FOR THOUGHT

SS-Obergruppenfuhrer Richard Walter Darre, a leading Nazi ideologist made a speech in 1940, expounding the fate of the British people assuming that the intended invasion of Britain proved successful.

"As soon as we beat England we shall make an end of all you Englishmen once and for all.

Able bodied men and women between the ages of 16 and 45 will be exported as slaves to the continent. The old and weak will be exterminated.

All men remaining in Britain as slaves will be sterilised and a million or two of the young women of nordic type will be segregated in a number of stud farms where, with the assistance of picked German sires, during a period of 10 or 12 years they will produce annually a series of nordic infants to be brought up in every way as Germans.

These infants will form the future population of Britain.

They will be educated in Germany and only those who fully satisfy the Nazi requirements will be allowed to return to Britain and take up permanent residence.

The rest will be sterilised and sent to join slave gangs in Germany.

In a generation or two, the British people will disappear."

Darre was captured in 1945 and tried for war crimes at the Nuremberg proceedings.

He was sentenced to 5 years in prison and was released in 1950. He died in Munich on September 5th 1983 aged 58.

About the Author

Roy Bartlett was born 1930 in the London borough of Ealing and has remained a resident throughout his life.

Married to wife Beryl for the past 51 years they have one son and two grandchildren.

Roy is well known in local sporting circles as the founder and ultimately president of Viking Sports football club which is famed for innovative and adventurous overseas tours-these include the Soviet Union and an ill-fated tour of Eastern Europe in 1968 when the club was caught up in the Russian led 'Warsaw Pact' invasion of Czechoslovakia. This dramatic episode was featured in an earlier book 'Let's Have a Ball'.

His current book 'A Little Boy's War' concludes where his sporting interests began at the end of the war in 1945.

Now aged 75 Roy suffers partial disablement as the long term effect of a leg injury sustained during the German Luftwaffe 'Blitz' on London in 1940.

Over a period of 60 years his involvement in many diverse community projects apart from sport, was recognised by inclusion in the 2001 'New Years Day London Roll of Honour' for ongoing service to the community of the London borough of Ealing.

Roy currently participates in a 'Reminiscence Roadshow' depicting wartime life which is presented to schools, senior citizen clubs and the like. He also works closely with the Gunnersbury Park Museum educational programme and has featured in the London Week-end Television series 'Blitz Spirit'

Printed in the United Kingdom
by Lightning Source UK Ltd.
112088UKS00001B/319-333